MW00773535

Jewish Perspectives on the New Testament

Jewish Perspectives on the New Testament

by *Victor Strazhnik*

Copyright © 2023 by Victor Strazhnik

Published by Victor Strazhnik

All rights reserved. No part of this publication may be reproduced, stored in a re-trieval system, or transmitted in any form or by any means—for example, electronic, photocopy, or recording—without the prior written permission of the publisher. The only exception is brief quotations in printed reviews.

Unless otherwise indicated, Scripture is taken from the New American Standard Bible, NASB, Copyright © 1977. Used by permission of Lockman Foundation, Inc., La Habra, CA 90632. All rights reserved.

Holy Bible, New International Version, NIV, Copyright © 1973, 1978, 1984 by International Bible Society. Used by permission of Zondervan. All rights reserved.

Christian Standard Bible, CSB, Copyright © 2017 by Holman Bible Publishers, One LifeWay Plaza, Nashville, TN 37234. Used by permission of Holman Bible Publish-ers. All rights reserved.

King James Version, 1611, 1769.

When needed, the translation is that of the author.

Library of Congress Cataloging-in-Publication Data is Available:

ISBN 979-8-218-03118-0
ISBN 979-8-218-03118-3 (ebook)

Cover design: Wonderstruck Arts

Contents

Introduction

Luke 22:70-71:

> [70] *And they all asked, "and are you the Son of God?"*
> *And he said to them, "You say that I am."*
> [71] *And they said, "What further need do we have of testimony?*
> *And we have heard it ourselves from His mouth."*

For those who are unfamiliar with the Law of Moses, the verse quoted above may seem to present the case of the Lord's confession in the rejection of the Law as the evidence for His condemnation to death. This calls for checking the context of the verse in the Old Testament as well as the context of all relevant verses in the four Gospels, which leads to some interesting discoveries.

1. The Mosaic Law (Ex. 23:1) prohibits conviction of a defendant on the basis of his testimony. The High Priest and all other members of the Sanhedrin purposefully broke the Law of Moses.
2. Mosaic Law (Lev. 19:15) prohibits unjust decisions by a judge (see Matt. 26:66).
3. The Law (Ex. 23:6) says: "do not kill the innocent and righteous" (see Matt. 26:66).
4. Only on the evidence of *two* or of *three* witnesses shall a charge be established (Deut. 19:15). It was none.
5. According to the Law (Deut. 13:14) "you must thoroughly inquire, probe and investigate." This was not done.
6. The Law states: "you shall do to a false witness as he had meant to do to his brother" (Deut. 19:15). Mosaic Law condemns the Sanhedrin to death.
7. The Law (Num. 35:12) prohibits beating before condemnation

by a judge's order (see John 18:22).

8. The Law (Num. 35:12) prohibits condemnation before deliberation by a judge (see John 18:22).

9. The Law (Ex. 20:13) prohibits false witnessing (see Matt. 26:59).

10. The Law (Lev. 10:6) prohibits priests to tear their clothing as demonstration of an emotional decision (see Mark 14:63).

Thus, *a few of commandments* of Mosaic Law were *deliberately* broken by members of the Sanhedrin. In this case the prosecutors are the ones guilty of the premeditated murder. They are the ones who do *not believe* in God.

This expanded interpretation of just two verses in the Gospel of Luke becomes possible by understanding that any verse in the New Testament can only be understood in its Biblical context, from the first words of the Book of Genesis to the final words of the Book of Revelation.

The concept of Jesus as the Messiah of Israel is emphasized in this work.

Exploration of the Jewish background of the New Testament theology contributes to a much fuller comprehension of the scriptural text and thus leads the reader to a deeper Christian faith.

As theologian and New Testament scholar Michael Bird writes: "To make Jesus 'Messiah' means that he can never be a heavenly redeemer who floated down to earth and teaching bad people how to be good and how to get to heaven. Jesus can only be the Savior of Gentiles, if he is first and foremost the Savior of Israel."[1]

---

1   Michael Bird, Jesus as Messiah: An Interview with Michael Bird (2009).

Main Definitions

The focus of this study is to equip seekers with foundational Biblical definitions of key terms. What follows may be obvious to some, but generally speaking the true definitions of these terms are not widely known.

Sin

Sin is based on man's disobedience to God in Gen. 3, and is an essential concept for understanding other Christian concepts and doctrines. The precise classical definition of sin is given in the New Testament (1 John 3:4): *"sin is without the Law."* Life in violation of and disobedience to the Law of Moses is sin. We find three conceptions of sin in the Old Testament:

1. *Unintentional sin*, which calls the sinner to make a sacrifice to atone for it; in our day, the prayer of repentance will suffice. Unknown sin also falls under this category and is defined as the sin of the unknown consequences of actions and decisions. In Biblical times, the sacrifice in the Holy of Holies was carried out on the Day of Atonement once per year.
2. *Intentional sin*. No sacrifices can atone for this. The only one way to redemption is sincere remorse.
3. *Intentional unbelief.* There is no atonement or sacrifice for this.

The teachings of the Mosaic Law will now be examined further.

Non-Biblical definitions of sin accepted in different Churches may result in a situation where one group acknowledges an act as sinful, while another accepts it as a normal or healthy behavior or lifestyle.

It is of the utmost importance to grasp that this misrepresentation of sin negatively affects the correct understanding of the concepts and definitions of righteousness, justification, and sanctification, as well as all other subordinate definitions or doctrines.

Generational Sin

Some believe in a generational sin, or generational curse, or generational spirits on the basis of a single Biblical verse (Ex. 20:5). Careful analysis provides a different perspective: this verse refers to the absolute right of God to destroy unbelievers together with their children, grandchildren, and great-grandchildren. Multitudes perished as the result of flood (Gen. 6-7) and of fire and brimstone in Sodom and Gomorrah (Gen. 19:24).

But this is not applicable to Israel, as stated in Ezek. 18:20:

> [20] "The person who sins will die. The son will not bear the punishment for the father's iniquity, nor will the father bear the punishment for the son's iniquity; the righteousness of the righteous will be upon himself, and the wickedness of the wicked will be upon himself."

Note that the verse in Ezek. 18:20 was given to Israel at least seven centuries after Ex. 20:5.

When believers do not desire to belong to Israel, or do not believe in Jesus as the Messiah of Israel, Biblical misinterpretation is inevitable.

Faith

Emuna is the Hebrew word for the Biblical faith, based on trust of God and obedience to His Law. *Emuna* calls for each person's behavior and character to be consistent with a stance of trust and reliance. Hence, one's works must serve as evidence to all observers; *emuna* is faith in action.

With this concept in mind, there is no contradiction when the same event and characters are referred to by two different authors in the New Testament.

James 2:21:

> [21] Was not our forefather Abraham justified by works when he led his son Isaac on the altar?

Heb. 11:17:

> [17] By faith Abraham, when God tested him, offered Isaac as a sacrifice.

Both authors allude to Gen. 22:1-8, but without understanding *emuna*, one might assume that they arrive at two different conclusions. With a correct grasp of *emuna*, however, we can see that Abraham is assuredly justified by his faith and by the evidence of his works.

Righteousness

The Hebrew word for righteousness is *tzedakah*. The Lord is righteous and perfect. His Laws are based on His own character and attributes. They constitute the plumb line by which He measures human righteousness. See Ps. 119:160:

> [160] The sum of your word is truth, and every one of your righteous rules endures forever.

The *only* definition of righteousness as such is given in Deut. 6:21, 23-25:

> [21] And you shall say to your son, we were slaves to Pharaoh in Egypt, and the Lord brought us from Egypt with a mighty hand... [23] And he brought us out from there to bring us in and give us the land that he promised on oath to our forefathers. [24] And the Lord commanded us to obey all these decrees, to fear the Lord our God, so that we might prosper in all days and be kept alive, as is the case today. [25] And that will be our *righteousness* if we are careful to obey all these commandments before the face of Lord our God, as he has commanded us.

Simply stated, being righteous is the condition necessary to reach heaven.

Those verses allow us to conclude the following:

- true believers always live in righteousness
- to be righteous is the command of God
- to be righteous is the believer's continuous condition

and refusing this command is a transgression of Mosaic Law.

As righteousness is incompatible with intentional sin, it is possible to lose it according to Ezek. 3:20-21:

> [20] And if a righteous man turns from his righteousness and does evil, and I put a stumbling block before him, he will die. Since you did not warn him, he will die for his sin. And the righteous things he did will not be remembered, and I will hold for his blood on your hand. [21] And if you do warn the righteous man that the righteous should not sin and he does not sin, he will live because he took warning, and you will have saved your soul.

Sanctification

Let us compare two approaches to describe a new believer's faith first, without applying the Law, and second, while taking the Law into account. Traditionally, the order of events is baptism, justification, sanctification. Paul described another order: baptism, sanctification, justification in 1 Cor. 6:9-11:

> [9] Do you not know that the unrighteous will not inherit the kingdom of God? Do not be deceived: Neither the sexually immoral nor idolaters nor adulterers nor male prostitutes nor homosexuals [10] nor thieves nor covetous nor drunkards nor slanderers nor swindlers will inherit the kingdom of God. [11] And that is what some of you were. But you were *washed*, but you were *sanctified*, but you were *justified* in the name of our Lord Jesus Christ and by the Spirit of our God.

According to Paul, unbelievers violate the Law of Moses; that is why they are unbelievers. He also states that all believers are righteous. Paul teaches that baptism, sanctification, and justification are synchronized as an all-in-one complete event.

It is worth noting that only four years passed between Paul's visit to Corinth and the subsequent writing of this letter. Some Corinthian Christians measured the time of their faith in *weeks*. Paul writes in 1 Cor 1:2:

> [2] To the ecclesia of God that is in Corinth, to those sanctified in Christ Jesus called to be holy, together with all those who call on the name of our Lord Jesus Christ, everywhere in their place and in our place.

He addressed all members of the Church in 2 Cor. 1:1 in the same manner.

For Paul the believers there were not *partially sanctified* or *semi-saints*; rather, he called the believers of Corinth sanctified and holy. Their sanctification was complete. The term "sanctification" means a process of being set apart by God. The first time it is used in the Bible in Gen. 2:3, where it refers to the Sabbath being sanctified. When the Jewish context of the New Testament is not applied, the concept of "being separated" is changed to "being sinless."

The term is used with this meaning throughout the Bible and has nothing to do with the ability to perform miracles.

In fact, Judaism does not require any perfection of people, but rather faith and submission to commands of the Law. Unlike Jews, Gentiles should observe only *some* of the Law commandments. Every believer is still imperfect, and still commits *unintentional* sins, but he or she is righteous, holy, and justified by faith and by keeping God's commandments. Jesus established exactly this order.

Thus, believers will stay sanctified and righteous for all of their lives. Of course, the process of the believer's journey to perfection should continue throughout their lives, but it does not affect the basic state of righteousness, justification, or holiness. This can be better understood with the following analogy: a white wall could be painted anew with white paint every day, but even if it is not, the color of the wall will not fundamentally change. One can also think of the concept of kosher food, i.e., "separate" or sanctified food; there is no such thing as half-kosher food: it is either kosher or not.

Another example of the concept of "being separated" is found in Num. 23:9:

> ...a people who dwells apart and shall not be reckoned among Gentiles.

The Jews were never "saints," but they were always a *separate* people. It is no accident that the following is written in the New Testament (Rev. 1:6):

> 6 and has made us to be a kingdom, *priests* to God and his Father, to him be glory and power for ever and ever, amen.

Believers are described as priests in the Temple because they, just like priests, are separated and dedicated to God.

A description of Gentile Christians in the New Testament can be found in 3 John 5-7:

> 5 Beloved, you are acting faithfully in what you are doing for the brothers, and strangers. 6 They have testified to the ecclesia about your love. You will do well to send them on their journey in a manner worthy of God. 7 It was for the sake of the Name that they went out, receiving no help from the Gentiles.

John fully supports the idea that one should not seek help from outsiders. Journeymen are Gentiles, literally "nations." But it means that neither the journeymen, nor those who send them, are Jews. John's way of thinking is simple: he continues to divide all people into "us" and "them" according to the Jewish culture. "We" are Israel, and "they" are "goyim," Gentiles. "We" believe in God, "they" do not believe in God. And because Gentile Christians are proselytes, John describes them as part of "us." Therefore, John accepts Gentile Christians as a part of Israel based on their faith in Jewish Messiah.

Sanctification in the Old Testament is described in Heb. 9:13:

> 13 And if the blood of goats, and bulls, and the ashes of a young cow, sprinkling those who are defiled, sanctify for the purification of the flesh...

As noted above, the whole of Israel was sanctified on the Day of Atonement every year.

Similarly, spouse and children are sanctified by the believer (1 Cor. 7:14):

> [14] And the unbelieving husband is made holy in the wife, and the unbelieving wife is made holy in the husband. Otherwise, your children would be unclean, and now they are holy.

Sanctification applies also to the people who have recently become believers and are still committing serious offenses (1 Thess. 4:3-7, 5:23):

> [4:3] And this is God's will, your sanctification: that you keep away from sexual immorality, [4] that each of you knows how to control his own body in holiness and honor, [5] not with lustful passions, like the Gentiles, who don't know God. [6] This means one must not transgress against and take advantage of a brother or sister in this manner, because the Lord is an avenger of all these offenses, as we also previously told and warned you. [7] And God has not called us to impurity but into holiness...
> [5:23] And may the God of peace himself sanctify you completely. And may your whole spirit, and soul, and body be kept sound and blameless at the coming of our Lord Jesus Christ.

Thus, it turns out that those who adhere to the idea of the necessity of the process of sanctification throughout their lives are falsely imputing their own problematic relationship with God to everybody else. By misinterpreting the meaning of sanctification, they bring the rest of believers into what the Bible says in Deut. 27:26: "Cursed be anyone who does not keep the words of this Law by doing them."

While the Biblical meaning of sanctification is "to be separated for God," some churches identify it as "to reach an uncertain but exceptionally high level of holiness." According to the Law of Moses this redefinition of the concept is a *deliberate violation* of the third of the Ten Commandments (Ex. 20:7): "Do not misuse the name of the Lord your God."

Biblically, it is *not an increase in holiness, but an increase in usefulness to other people*. And such usefulness might indeed increase indefinitely.

Justification

If sin is defined as a breach of the Law, righteousness is defined by its acceptance. As the commandments of the Law are given by God out of love and mercy, their observance is also based on love in response to the grace of God. Ultimately, it is God who determines man's righteousness within His framework of conduct. The concept of righteousness does not differ in the Old and the New Testaments; it is the same righteousness, which is manifested in different ways in different circumstances. Justification is a way of declaring somebody a righteous person.

Considering the Jewish background of the New Testament, and consequently the legitimacy of the Mosaic Law, allows us to achieve critical Biblical knowledge. It is similar to the transition from vague and uncertain images in twilight to the bright, clear, and pleasant images of daylight. It becomes apparent why Apostle Paul wrote in Rom 2:13-14:

> [13] And it is not those who hear the Law who are righteous before God, but it is those who obey the Law will be righteous. [14] And when Gentiles, who do not have the Law, do by nature things required by the Law, they are a Law for themselves, though they do not have the Law...

This verse demonstrates Paul's understanding of Scriptures, especially Gen. 15:6:

> [6] And Abraham believed the Lord, and he credited it to him as righteousness.

Abraham lived long before Moses, so he could not hear the Law.[2] Nevertheless, he kept the Law. Obviously, it was not the whole Law, but some commandments.

---

2   Scot McKnight, The Letter of James (2011) 245-256.

In short, *the Law of Moses is God's measure of man's existence in righteousness.*

By itself the Law does not have the power for justification and salvation and cannot declare a man righteous.

The word "righteousness" in Hebrew means the right and balanced relationship with God. Lack of righteousness then is a disruption of the balance in the relationship with God. Thus, justification is the establishment of a right relationship with God. The fact proves the impossibility of being righteous and remaining unjustified. Thus, it is logical to conclude that a person is justified at the moment of making a decision to believe in God.

Because *all* believers are justified, all nonbelievers are not justified. This is a scarlet thread running through the whole New Testament, where believers are either declared to have completed the process of sanctification (Acts 26:18; Rom. 6:19, 22, 15:16; 1 Cor. 1:2, 6:11; Eph. 5:26; 1 Tim. 4:5; 2 Tim. 2:21; Heb. 2:11, 10:10, 10:14, 10:29, 13:12; 1 Peter 3:15; Jude 1; Rev. 22:11) or they are addressed as saints (Acts 3:21, 9:13, 9:32, 9:41, 26:10; Rom. 1:7, 8:27, 11:16, 12:13, 15:25, 15:26, 15:31, 16:2, 16:15; 1 Cor. 1:2, 6:1, 6:2, 14:33, 16:1, 16:15; 2 Cor. 1:1, 8:4, 9:1, 9:12, 13:13; Eph. 1:1, 1:4, 1:15, 1:18, 2:19, 2:21, 3:5, 3:8, 3:18, 4:12, 5:3, 5:27, 6:18; Phil. 1:1, 4:21, 4:22; Col. 1:2, 1:4, 1:12, 1:26, 3:12; 1 Thess. 3:13, 5:27; 2 Thess. 1:10; 1 Tim. 5:10; Phil. 5, 7; Heb. 3:1, 6:10, 12:10, 13:24; 1 Peter 1:15, 1:16, 2:9, 3:5; 2 Peter 1:21, 3:2; Jude 3, 14; Rev. 5:8, 8:3, 8:4, 11:18, 13:7, 13:10, 14:12, 15:3, 16:6, 17:6, 18:24, 19:8, 20:6, 20:9, 22:6, 22:11) or they are called righteous (Matt. 10:41, 25:37; Rom. 5:19; James 5:16; 1 John 2:29, 3:7).

Salvation

All denominations, including Messianic, and pseudo-Christian cults, proclaim Jesus as the savior of all nations. Gentile believers receive salvation from God, who *created* the Jewish people. They are grafted into the Jewish olive tree of faith becoming part of Israel. However, there are multiple teachings that either do not refer to Jesus as the Jewish Messiah or say exactly the opposite.

We find a reference to the Old Testament in Heb. 4:2:

> [2] And we heard the gospel [in the first century A.D.] just as they [unbelievers in the thirteenth century B.C.], but the message they heard did not benefit them, because they were not united by faith in those who heard.

See also 1 Cor. 10:1, 4:

> [1] For I do not want you to be ignorant of the fact, brothers, that our forefathers were all under the cloud and that they all passed through the sea...
> [4] and all drank the same spiritual drink, and they were drinking from the spiritual rock that accompanied them, and that rock was Christ.

All people who came out of Egypt not only had *seen* Jesus but had also *heard* Him giving the same Gospel of salvation. This means that the exact same salvation was available to people in the Old Testament. Thus, the teachings of the nineteenth and twentieth centuries, on salvation being obtained in seven different ways at different times or dispensations, are contradicted by the Bible.

Luke's Gospel complements the reasoning from Heb 4:2. See Luke 1:6:

> [6] And they [the priest Zechariah and his wife] were both *righteous* in the sight of God, walking *blamelessly* in all the commandments and requirements of the Lord.

Therefore, *prior* to the start of Jesus' ministry, some people already believed in Him and *kept* the Law of Moses, and they were saved just like the recent followers of Jesus.

The Apostle Paul wrote about how people were saved *before* Israel left Egypt, and *prior* receiving the Law (Rom 1:19-20):

> [1:19] For what can be known about God is evident to them, and God has shown it to them. [20] For his invisible attributes, namely, his eternal power and divine nature, have been clearly perceived, in

the things that have been made since the creation of the world. So, they are without excuse.

See also Rom. 2:14-15:

> [2:14] And when Gentiles, who do not have the Law, by nature do what the Law requires, they are the Law to themselves, though they do not have the Law, [15] since they show that the requirements of the Law are written on their hearts, their consciences also bearing witness, and their thoughts after one another accusing, and defending them.

Thus, any attempt to find a loophole for unbelievers to ignore the Biblical message drives them further from knowing God and His Law.

Salvation is a gift from God, not a payment (Rom. 3:23-24):

> [23] and all have sinned and fall short of the glory of God, [24] and are justified by his grace as a gift.

Is it possible to lose salvation? See Ezek. 18:21-24:

> [21] "And if the wicked man turns from all his sins which he has committed and observes all My statutes and practices justice and righteousness, he shall surely live; he shall not die. [22] "All his transgressions which he has committed will not be remembered against him; because of his righteousness which he has practiced, he will live. [23] "Do I have any pleasure in the death of the wicked," declares the Lord God, "rather than that he should turn from his ways and live? [24] "And when a righteous man turns away from his righteousness, commits iniquity, and does according to all the abominations that a wicked man does, will he live? All his righteous deeds which he has done will not be remembered for his treachery which he has committed and his sin which he has committed; for them he will die.

The same idea is reflected in James 5:19-20 and Heb. 6:4-6.

All arguments about predestination and freedom of choice are moot.

The statement from Pirkei Avot[3] teaches (3:15):

> [15] Everything is foreseen yet freedom of choice is granted, And the world is judged with goodness; And everything is in accordance with the preponderance of works.

Ecclesia of Jesus

The word *ecclesia* is used ninety-one times in the Old Testament in Septuagint, and it stands for a congregation of the called people.

As the Old Testament is written by Jewish authors, it almost always refers to the *ecclesia* of Israel, or the assembly of Israel.

The nation of Israel was created by God, who calls for a special relationship. In the Old Testament eight instances of the expression "the Lord's ecclesia" (*kahal Yehovah* in Hebrew) are found in Deut. 23:1, 23:2, 23:3, 23:8; Judg. 20:2, 1 Chron. 29:20; Neh. 13:1; Mic. 2:5.

In the New Testament, this expression is translated twelve times as "ecclesia of God" in Acts 20:28; 1 Cor 1:2, 10:32, 11:16, 11:22, 15:9; 2 Cor 1:1, 8:1; 1 Thess. 2:14; 2 Thess. 1:4; 1 Tim. 3:5, 3:15.

In addition, we find the expression "synagogue of the Jews" in the New Testament (Acts 17:1, 10, 17). In the Old Testament LXX it is reasonable to expect "ecclesia of the Jews" (Est. 4:16). Notably, the Greek word "synagogue" corresponds to the Hebrew word *eda*.

The expression "ecclesia of the saints" is used in both the Old and New Testaments (Ps. 89:5, 149; 1 Cor. 14:33). In addition, we find "holy ecclesia" in Joel 2:16. The expression was not taken into account when the definition of the word "holiness" was changed from "to be separated for God" to "to work miracles" in the history of the Church. Consequently, ordinary believers are not aware that they are saints, but instead they frequently consider themselves to be sinners.

Having found the phrases "ecclesia of Israel" and "synagogue of Israel," one may expect some similarity between them. In Prov. 5:14

---

3   Pirkei Avot consists of the Mishnaic tractate of Avot, the second-to-last tractate in the order of Nezikin in the Mishnah.

(Hebrew text) the negligent student was almost completely disgraced in the midst of the *ecclesia* and the synagogue. According to Hebrew the words "ecclesia" and "synagogue" denote the same thing, and thus in this instance create a doubling effect to amplify the meaning.

It is also good to remember that the Church can be a synagogue, as it says in James 2:2:

> ² And if a man comes into your synagogue wearing a golden ring and shining white clothes, and a poor man in old shabby clothes also comes in.

The words "synagogue" and "ecclesia" (James 5:14) correspond to the meaning of these words *eda*⁴ and *kahal*⁵ in Hebrew. Notably, *kahal* was translated into Greek as *ecclesia* on two out of three occasions, but also as synagogue in one instance.

Finally, in the New Testament, the *ecclesia* is made of Jews and Gentiles. *In the Old Testament the ecclesia also is made of Jews and Gentiles.* We read in 2 Chron. 30:25 that Israel and *HaGerim* are listed together, where the latter are the aliens who have joined Israel and comprise one community.

Tikkun olam: Repairing the World

In Judaism, the prayer Aleynu calls for faith and for repairing the world. The prayer includes the phrase *tikkun olam b'malchut shaddai*, translated as "when the world shall be perfected under the reign of the Almighty." Jesus' work exemplifies it. Some Jewish interpreters bring the definition of *tikkun olam* as repair of the world or the just society, where people are God's senior partners. But in Hebrew, one can arrive at this misleading meaning simply by adding the definite article "ha": *tikkun ha-olam*.

The Moab covenant as well as the New Testament are given by God as

---

4   The word *sunagoge,* which is used by Jews to denote their communities, has been used to translate the OT word *edah* 130 times.

5   In the LXX, *ekklesia* is used to translate the Hebrew word *qahal* seventy-three times out of a total of 123 occurrences, and as *sunagoge* thirty-five times.

tikkun olam to correct the relationship between Him and the people. It is easy to see that the most necessary part of any society, which is so often catastrophically missing, is the faith in God and love for one's neighbor.

The word *tikkun* only occurs four times in the Old Testament. See Ecc. 1:15:

> [15] What is crooked cannot be made *straight*, and what is lacking cannot be counted.

Ecc. 7:13:

> [13] Consider the work of God: who can *straighten* what he has made crooked?

Ecc. 12:9:

> [9] He listened and searched out and *straighten* many proverbs.

Dan. 4:36:

> ...and I was *reestablished* in my kingdom.

It is evident from these quotations that the term *tikkun olam* as such is not used in the Bible, though the concept occurs quite often, as in Matt. 5:17-19:

> [17] "Do not think that I have come to abolish the Law or the Prophets. I have not come to abolish them but to fulfill them. [18] I tell you the truth, until heaven and earth disappear, not the smallest letter, not the least stroke will disappear from the Law until everything is accomplished. [19] And anyone who *loosens* one of the least of these commandments and teaches others to do the same will be called least in the kingdom of heaven, and whoever practices and teaches these commands will be called great in the kingdom of heaven.

This brings out the most authentic, genuine meaning of *tikkun olam*.

In Hebrew, to "loose" the commandments of the Law means to break or annul the commandment, while to "tie" means to keep or to strengthen it.

First Commandment

The early history of the Church includes the progression from the Apostolic tradition to Emperor Constantine the Great's domestic Church. At this time the original first commandment lost its status and turned into the introduction to the Decalogue. Meanwhile it is still listed as the first commandment in the Hebrew Bible; to maintain the appearance of ten commandments, the second was divided into two commandments by different Christian denominations (Ex 20:3-6).

At first glance the First commandment is impossible to fulfill. It is not a commandment of works, but rather the affirmation of faith. In the same way, *Shema Israel*, "Hear, O Israel," which is read every day, is not a prayer, but the affirmation of faith (Deut. 6:4-5). Many Christians, on the other hand, do not feel any connection with the exodus from Egypt and being part of Israel.

Nevertheless, the First commandment is applied to all believers. The Jews believe that the souls of the people who are converted to Judaism have been present with the rest of Israel on Mount Sinai when Moses received the Ten Commandments. Also, in the rite of conversion to Judaism, Gentiles accept Abraham as their own ancestor. Therefore, Jesus, as well as all authors of the New Testament's books, include all Gentile Christians in Israel. Following this analogy, God brought each of them out of their own personal Egypt to faith. The prophet Amos taught that other nations besides Israel were also led by God through their own Exodus experiences (Amos 9:7).

But in Christianity the First commandment is regarded just as a statement, not as the commandment. For example, the modified first commandment differs from the original: "Thou shalt have no other gods before me." When Jews made the list of all 613 commandments, they could have arranged them in many ways. But regardless how they are grouped, this commandment always stays the first. That is probably why the First commandment was lost. At the first glance, this commandment seems quite harmless (Ex. 20:2):

> [2] "I am the Lord your God, who brought you out of the land of Egypt, out of the house of slavery."

Out of the 613 commandments, 612 delineate what to do or not to do. But the First commandment has nothing to do with people's behavior, and the whole Law of Moses is built on it. The Mosaic Covenant was based on the promise. The First commandment stated that the Law was established when this promise had become a reality. Those facts cannot be changed or "interpreted" differently such that they are declared to be fake. Unfortunately, they could be disregarded.

This commandment has been already fulfilled by God. God called Israel, presenting Himself: "I am the Lord." In English, the word "Lord" does not have the same timeless meaning as the phrase in Hebrew. Then He stated "I am your God." Notably, God did not ask Israel's opinion or give Israel a choice. This is the second fact. Fact number three: "I brought you out of the land of Egypt." This is followed by fact number four: "I brought you out of the house of slavery."

Four facts, and not a single punishment or reward or any hint of a temporary nature of the commandment. It is simply the statement that the God of Israel cares about them.[6]

The First commandment establishes and institutionalizes God's relationship with Israel. Such a commandment, with every word, contradicts the claim that the Law of Moses is abolished either completely or partially or temporally. Consequently, those who do not accept the First commandment break two other commandments: not to add anything to the Bible and not to take anything out from it. These commandments, quoted by the Apostle John (from the Old Testament), conclude the Bible (Rev. 22:18-19).

The First commandment is given by Jesus Christ Himself (1 Cor. 10:1-4, 9):

> [1] And I do not want you to be ignorant, brothers, that our forefathers were all under the cloud and that they all passed through the sea. [2] They were all *baptized* into Moses in the cloud and in the sea. [3] They all ate the same spiritual food [4] and drank the same spiritual drink, and they drank from the spiritual rock that walked with them, and that rock was *Christ*...

---

6   Brief, simple, good and competent explanation of the Ten Commandments is given on the pages Joseph Telushkin, Jewish literacy (2010) 40-42.

⁹ And we should not test the *Christ*, as some of them did and were killed by snakes.

The verses assist believers who struggle with understanding the one triune God (rather than three different gods). The same presence is described in John 14:23:

²³ Jesus answered and said to him: if anyone loves me, he will keep My word, and My Father will love him, and *we* will come and abode with him.

The absence of the First commandment in various denominations is indicative of the influence of Replacement Theology. The outcome is evident: when the Church does not feel itself to be part of Israel, it does not apply the First commandment. Without the First commandment, of course, there is no Law and Covenant with Israel. All of this leads to the loss of blessings and the gain of the new obstacles in one's relationship with God. We can see more on this outcome in Paul's letter to the Romans.

The history of the First commandment starts with the most significant event in Jewish history, the exodus from Egypt (Ex. 3) and the story of the burning bush. Even when the events of the exodus had not yet taken place and Jews were still slaves in Egypt, all parts of the First Commandment had already been given (Ex. 6:7):

⁷ and I *will* take you as my own people, and I *will* be your God, and you *will* know that I am the Lord your God, who *has brought* you out from under the yoke of the Egyptians.

In Ex. 20:2 the process was complete:

² I *am* the Lord your God, who *brought* you...

One may find multiple references to the First Commandment throughout the Bible. More than two hundred of them are found in the Pentateuch and the Prophets. In the New Testament one important instance stands out (1 Peter 1:15-16): "Be holy, because I am holy." The context of this quotation, found in Ex. 19:5-6; Lev. 11:44-45, 19:2-3, states that the righteousness of Christians is defined by the Law and based on the First commandment.

See Matt. 22:32, 37-40:

> [32] I am the God of Abraham, the God of Isaac, and the God of Jacob? He is not the God of the dead but of the living...
> [37] Jesus said: Love the Lord your God with all your heart and with all your soul and with all your mind. [38] This is the first and greatest commandment. [39] And the second is like it: Love your neighbor as yourself. [40] All the Law and the Prophets hang on these two commandments.

There are some people who believe that Jesus chose for His Church only these two commandments to keep. However, Jesus is the God of Abraham, Isaac, and Jacob. He is the God of Israel and in those verses Jesus answers the Pharisees regarding the two commandments that Pharisees themselves do not keep (Matt. 22:37, 22:39). His opinion about the Pharisees who asked Him is given in Matt. 23:1-36.

In short, the Law is founded on the faith of God Himself, and the First commandment becomes its foundation.

Trinity

The word Trinity originates in the Platonic term *trias*, or "three." This term was Latinized as *trinitas*, and later as the English word "Trinity." Believers have wrestled with some popular metaphors and analogies to explain the Trinity, such as "three states of water: ice, liquid, vapor" or "three components of an egg." These explanations ultimately fail because they use different properties, or substances, or objects.

God manifested Himself in a human body. The Creator incarnated in His creation. It is very difficult and confusing for a finite being to understand the infinite; in addition, both the Semitic way of reasoning and the Hebrew language itself present additional difficulties for understanding.

Jewish and Gentiles believers understand the Trinity differently. For Gentiles it is closer to the illustration on the left, where each Person of the Trinity has truly little in common with the other two.

For the Jewish believer, it is more like the illustration on the right. The differences between the three Persons of the Trinity are noticeable, but not significant; it is an attempt to approach God whose oneness is complex.

Using Hebrew grammar with the category of words which present *singular in plural*, we find Hebraic words with plural endings being used with singular verbs and adjectives (Gen. 1:26).

For example, the word God, singular, in Hebrew elohim, אֱלֹהִים, the plural of El. See Gen. 1:1:

> [1] In the beginning God [Elohim] created the heavens and the earth.

A good example of singular in plural is the word "life," khaiyim, ח''ם. Everyone has only one life, but the life of a one-day-old baby is not comparable with the life of a fifty-year-old. A married woman's life differs from the life of an unmarried teenage boy, a student's life is not the same as the life of a retiree, and so on. Those lives in plural are quite different, but these are parts of the same person's life, in singular. It is thought-provoking enough that the Hebrew words for sky (*mayim*) and water (*shamayim*) are both singular in plural.

Is it possible to understand the Trinity without Hebrew? One pastor shared that he was watching the sunrise over Yokohama Bay in Japan. Changing light conditions, colors of sky and water gave him some instinctive illustration of Trinity. The same sky over the water off the coast of Iceland would look hugely different.

Elohim

In trying to find proof of the Trinity in the Old Testament, believers refer to Gen. 1:26 (NASB):

> 26 Then God [Elohim] said, "Let *Us* make man in *Our* image, according to *Our* likeness...

This quotation strongly suggests the idea of the Trinity, as should be obvious to everybody. Nevertheless, all New Testament authors, despite their deep knowledge of the Old Testament, never referred to this quotation.

The word *Elohim*, with and without the definite article, occurs 1,046 times in the Old Testament and means in Hebrew "the being with a power over." Correctness of the meaning in every occurrence may be verified against the Septuagint. The name Elohim is used to describe the one true God (Ex 20:2):

> 2 I am the Lord your God [Elohim], who brought you out of Egypt, out of the land of slavery.

Compare the verse of Ex. 20:2 with all the applications of this word in the examples below.

False gods (Ex 20:3):

> 3 Do not have other gods [Elohim] besides me.Angels (Ps 8:5):
> 5 You made him a little lower than the angels [Elohim] and crowned him with glory and honor.

Judges (Ex 22:9):

> 9 In all cases of illegal possession of an ox, a donkey, a sheep, a garment, or any other lost property about which somebody says, 'This is mine,' both parties are to bring their cases before the judges [Elohim]. The one whom the judges [Elohim] declare guilty must pay back double to his neighbor.

Supernatural spirit (1 Sam. 28:13):

> 13 The king said to her, "Do not be afraid. What do you see?" And

the woman said to Saul, "I see a being [Elohim] coming up out of the earth." He said to her, "What is his appearance?" And she said, "An old man is coming up, and he is wrapped in a robe." And Saul knew that it was Samuel.

Thus, the word Elohim in Gen. 1:26 most probably means celestial beings. At times it is difficult to translate; see, for example Gen. 23:6:

> ⁶ "Sir, listen to us. You are a mighty [Elohim] chieftain among us.

It is critical to discern the usage meaning "the being with a power" versus "one true God." The Bible demonstrates the plural concept of God, called Elohim, without losing the sight of the singular YHWH.

Holy Spirit

The Holy Spirit is first mentioned in the Bible's second sentence, Gen. 1:2, as *ruach* in Hebrew. *Ruach* means breath, wind, Spirit, or an "essence." God's Ruach is the source of life.

Problematically, the King James Bible was presented as the only translation inspired by God, and in this translation Holy Spirit was translated as "spirit of God," with a lower case. Meanwhile Ex. 31:3, 35:31, Num. 24:2 are translated as "Spirit of God." When Gen. 1:2 is referred to in Acts 16:6, this is translated as "Holy Ghost." Thus, the KJV translation created a false impression of different Holy Spirits.

The presence of the Holy Spirit in the Old Testament is presented in the following verses.

Judg. 13:25:

> ²⁵ and the Spirit of the Lord began to stir him while he was in Mahaneh Dan, between Zorah and Eshtaol.

1 Sam. 11:6:

> ⁶ When Saul heard their words, the Spirit of God came upon him in power.

Ezek. 11:5:

> [5] Then the Spirit of the Lord came upon me, and He told me to say: "This is what the Lord says: That is what you are saying, O house of Israel, but I know what is going through your mind.

Similarly, the New Testament describes the work of Holy Spirit in various texts.

Acts 10:44:

> [44] While Peter was still saying these things, the Holy Spirit fell on all who heard the word.

Acts 11:15:

> [15] As I began to speak, the Holy Spirit fell on them just as on us at the beginning.

The Holy Spirit works in a similar way in the Old and the New Testaments.

As shown in the verses below, the Holy Spirit interacted with people in the Old Testament as He never did in the New Testament. For example, a few people were clothed in the Holy Spirit (Judg. 6:34):

> [34] But the Spirit of the Lord clothed Gideon, and he sounded the shofar.

See also 1 Chron. 12:18:

> [18] Then the Spirit clothed Amasai, chief of the thirty, and he said, "We are yours, O David, and with you, O son of Jesse! Peace, peace to you, and peace to your helpers! For your God helps you."

2 Chron. 24:20:

> [20] Then the Spirit of God clothed Zechariah the son of Jehoiada the priest, and he stood above the people, and said to them, "Thus says God, why do you break the commandments of the Lord, so that you cannot prosper? Because you have forsaken the Lord, he has forsaken you."

The Holy Spirit dwells in *each* believer in the New Testament, which is a new stage in the relationship between God and His people.

Will of God

The Biblical source for the description of the will of God was known for almost three thousand years (Ezek. 18:30-32):

> [30] So, *house of Israel*, I will judge you, each one according to his ways, declares the Sovereign Lord. Repent and turn away from all your transgressions, and iniquity will not be a stumbling block to you. [31] Cast away from you all your transgressions which you have committed, and make yourselves a new heart and a new spirit. And why will you die, house of Israel? [32] For I take no pleasure in the death of anyone who dies, declares the Lord God. *And repent and live*!

The outcome of the action is found in Ezek. 11:19, 33:30-32, 36:26, where it is clear that the will of God should be sought by all Gentile believers as they are adopted into Israel based on their faith in the Jewish Messiah.

God wants all Jews to return to Him. Sadly, God's will is not pursued in most cases. Various Churches use the following reasons to explain why they fail to follow God's will:

- Jewish evangelism is too costly and resources are limited.
- Jews are already saved by their birthright.
- Jews have already irrevocably lost their salvation.
- Jews cannot be saved in any circumstances.
- God temporarily suspended the salvation of Jews.
- God does not want Christians to be engaged in the salvation of Jews.
- Jews are needed to show the wrath of God. If they are saved, who would be the example of the wrath of God?
- This should not be the goal for Christians.
- Churches are not equipped with knowledge of Jewish evangelism.
- Saving Jews is too difficult.

- If Jews are saved, the Church would lose its non-Jewish character.
- Jewish evangelism should be left only for the Jewish believers to pursue.
- The priority is to bring Gentiles to faith.
- Jews are incompatible with Christianity and unable to become Christians.
- Jews are guilty of the crucifixion of our Lord.

Of course, God's word was well known to the Jews in the time of the apostles (Acts 13:5, 14:1):

> 13:5 When they arrived at Salamis, *they proclaimed the word of God in the Jewish synagogues*. John was with them as their helper...
>
> 14:1 At Iconium Paul and Barnabas went *as usual* into the Jewish synagogue. There they spoke so effectively that a great number of Jews and Gentiles believed.

And Apostle Paul confirms the same truth about God in Rom. 11:11:

> 11 And I say: Did they stumble so as to fall? Not at all! But because of their transgression, *salvation has come to the Gentiles to make them [Jews] envious*.

Creation of Israel

Abraham (originally Abram), the founding father of the nation, is referred to as a Hebrew in Gen. 14:13 for the first time. The Hebrews are called the chosen people, *created* by God as described in the Bible. He used them to bring His Law and the Savior to the world.

It was more than a struggle for Abram to trust the following impossible promise (Gen. 12:2):

> 2 "I will make you into a great nation and I will bless you; I will make your name great, and you will be a blessing.

After that Abram began to doubt God's ability to deliver (Gen. 15:4):

> 4 Then the word of the Lord came to him: "This man will not be

your heir, but a son coming from your own body will be your heir."

Finally, Abraham began to laugh in Gen. 17:17, 21, but God did not retreat from His promise:

> [17] Abraham fell facedown; he laughed and said to himself, "Will a son be born to a man a hundred years old? Will Sarah bear a child at the age of ninety?"...
> [21] But my covenant I will establish with Isaac, whom Sarah will bear to you by this time next year."

Of course, Sarah didn't believe God either (Gen. 18:12):

> [12] So Sarah laughed to herself as she thought, "After I am worn out and my master old, will I now have this pleasure?"

But God has the last word (Gen. 21:2-3):

> [2] Sarah became pregnant and bore a son to Abraham in his old age, at the very time God had promised him. [3] Abraham gave the name Isaac to the son Sarah bore him.

And eventually Isaac asked God for exactly the same miracle (Gen. 25:21):

> [21] Isaac prayed to the Lord on behalf of his wife, because she was barren. The Lord answered his prayer, and his wife Rebekah became pregnant.

Thus, the Jewish people came into being as the direct outcome of God's involvement in these two miracles. The Bible narrates the special and unique connection of God with the Jewish nation.

Messiah of Israel

Luke recorded the account of Jesus telling His disciples to be the Messiah promised in the Old Testament (Luke 24:44-47). Salvation is given through faith in Jesus in accordance with the Old and New Testaments. The Holy Spirit was with believers also in Biblical times. In the New Testament God revealed Himself as the Messiah of Israel, as well as the Messiah of all nations.

The term "Messiah," מָשִׁיחַ, existed since Old Testament times, when it was applied only to Israel. It is first used in Psalm 2:2, where the Messiah is the Savior of Israel and the judge of the Gentiles.

> ² And the kings of the earth take their stand, and the rulers take counsel together against the Lord and His Messiah.

The first man to recognize Jesus as the Messiah of Israel was Simeon (Luke 2:25-32, 36, 38):

> ²⁵ And there was a man in Jerusalem, whose name was Simeon, and this man was righteous and devout, waiting for the consolation of Israel, and the Holy Spirit was upon him. ²⁶ And it had been revealed to him by the Holy Spirit that he would not see death before he had seen the Lord's Christ.²⁸ And he took him up in his arms, and blessed God, and said, ²⁹ Lord, now you are letting your servant depart in peace, according to your word; ³⁰ for my eyes have seen your salvation ³¹ that you have prepared in the presence of all peoples, ³² a light for revelation to the Gentiles, and for glory to your people Israel...
> ³⁶ And there was a prophetess, Anna, the daughter of Phanuel, of the tribe of Asher. She was advanced in years, having lived with her husband seven years from when she was a virgin...
> ³⁸ And at that very hour she came up and began to give thanks to God and to speak of him to all who were waiting for the redemption of Jerusalem.

Luke explains that Simeon, who was keeping the Law and being righteous, had the Holy Spirit upon him, and was saved. The prophetess Anna came from the so-called "lost" ten tribes of Israel and was righteous, as are all prophets of God. When the Messiah was revealed to her, she told everyone about Him.

But before that, there were shepherds in Luke 2:8, 10-11, 16-18:

> ²:⁸ And there were shepherds living out in the fields nearby, keeping watch over their flock at night...
> ¹⁰ And the angel said to them...¹¹ Today in the town of David a Savior has been born to you, he is Christ the Lord...
> ⁶ And they hurried off, and found Mary and Joseph, and the baby,

who was lying in the trough. [17] And they had seen him, they spread the word concerning what had been told them about this child, [18] and all who heard it were amazed at what the shepherds said to them.

Andrew was the first disciple to proclaim Jesus (John 1:41):

[41] The first thing Andrew did was to find his brother Simon and tell him, "We have found the Messiah," which is translated Christ.

Then Nathanael said in John 1:49:

[49] Answered Nathanael: "Rabbi, you are the Son of God; you are the King of Israel."

Apostle Peter declared Jesus as the Messiah of Israel (Matt. 16:16):

[16] And Simon Peter answered, "You are the Christ, the Son of the living God."

Three Parts of Israel

In the Moab Covenant (Deut. 29), God defined Israel as being comprised of three groups:

1. Unbelieving Jews
2. Believing Jews
3. Gentile believers

The first group was the most prominent during their stay in Sinai desert upon entering the Promised Land, but the second and the third groups *always* existed.

One of the Biblical narratives of the second group can be found in 1 Kings 19:13-14:

[13] And when Elijah heard it, and he wrapped his face in his cloak, and went out, and stood at the entrance of the cave. And there came a voice to him, and said, "What are you doing here, Elijah?" [14] And he said, "I have been very jealous for the Lord, the God of hosts. For the people of Israel have forsaken your covenant,

thrown down your altars, and killed your prophets with the sword, and *only* I left, and they seek my life, to take it away."

And God answered Elijah in 1 Kings 19:18:

> [18] And I will leave *seven thousand* in Israel, all the knees that have not bowed to Baal, and every mouth that has not kissed him.

Whatever the circumstances and the first group being the majority of the nation, God *never* forsakes Israel, and He continues to take care of her faithful remnant.

The personality of Jesus is inextricably linked to Israel. Paul admits this in Rom. 1:16-17:

> [1:16] And I am not ashamed of the gospel, for it is the power of God for salvation to everyone who believes, both, *firstly* to the Jew and to the Greek. [17] And in it the righteousness of God is revealed real faith, as it is written, "And the righteous shall live by faith."

The word "firstly," in Greek "proton," in the absence of the following enumeration means *priority*. But that priority entails a great responsibility (Rom. 2:9-10):

> [2:9] There will be tribulation and distress for every human being who does evil, both, *firstly* to the Jew and to the Greek, [10] and glory, and honor, and peace for everyone who does good, both, *firstly* to the Jew and to the Greek.

According to Biblical narrative Israel as the nation belongs to God (Rom. 15:8-10):

> [15:8] And I tell you that Christ became a servant to the circumcised to show God's truthfulness, in order to confirm the promises given to the forefathers, [9] and in order that the Gentiles might glorify God for his mercy. As it is written, "Therefore I will praise you among the Gentiles, and sing to your name." [10] And again it is said, "Rejoice, Gentiles, with his people."

At all times, Jesus continues to care about Jewish people.

Salvation of Israel

Apostle Paul wrote about the priority of Israel's salvation in

Rom. 11:1-2, 11, 14, 16:

> [11:1] And I ask, then, has God rejected his people? By no means! And I myself am an Israelite, a descendant of Abraham, a member of the tribe of Benjamin. [2] God has not rejected his people whom he foreknew...
> [11] And I ask, did they [Jews] stumble in order that they might fall? By no means! Rather, through their trespass salvation has come to the Gentiles, to make Israel jealous...
> [14] if somehow I might move to envy my own people and save some of them...
> [16] And if the first piece is holy, everything is also, and if the root is holy, the branches are too.

The Old Testament describes two houses: Judah and Israel. The New Testament commentators present two houses: Israel and the Church, while there should be the only one. The first time the Bible's readers learn about it from Jesus Himself (Matt. 15:24):

> [24] And He answered and said, I was sent only to the lost sheep of the house of Israel.

And again in John 10:16:

> [16] And I have other sheep, which are not of this fold, I must bring them also, and they shall hear My voice, and they shall become one flock and one shepherd.

So, it should be *one* herd, where Gentiles unite with Israel.

In reality, using the teachings of the first and second Nicene Councils (325 and 787 A.D.)[7] to create a united community of Jews and Gentiles in the Church over the past two thousand years has not been successful, as was forcefully demonstrated by James Parkes in the year 1934.[8]

---

7   Second Council of Nicaea, Canon 8.

8   James Parkes, *The Conflict of the Church and Synagogue: A Study in the Origins of Anti-Semitism* (1934).

Semitic Logic

The authors of the New Testament wrote in Greek but reasoned and thought in their native Hebrew. Some scholars believe that Luke was a Jew based on an analysis of his writing style, use of Hebrew idioms, and Semitic reasoning.

Semitic people love analogy and use it very often. For them, analogy is one of the methods of logical and legal proof. In the Bible, analogy brings together individual events or sentences that would remain separate in all other modes of thinking. Jesus often used analogy in the form of a parable, and God the Father used analogy to interact with people. In the Jewish mind, descriptions of the miracle are often crafted in this form.

In Jewish reasoning, the analogy is similar to a stack of sheets of translucent paper. It is obvious that the entire stack is made up of separate layers, and that the top layer is not the same as the bottom. On the other hand, they all form a pattern that is accepted as a complete unit. In the Letter to Hebrews, the author argued for five such layers (3:7-4:11).

Alfred Edersheim in 1883 was first who described this type of reasoning to English speaking Christians.[9] The best explanation of Semitic logic, in the author's opinion, is given in Moses Mielziner, *Introduction to the Talmud* (1894) pp. 130-152.

Kal Vachomer

"Kal Vachomer" as a rule of Semitic logic presents a challenge to Gentile believers. It is the logical inference based on the relative compar-

---

9   Alfred Edersheim, The Life and Times of Jesus the Messiah, Volume 2 (1883) 285.

ison of elements and loosely translates "from easy to heavy" or "from simple to complex." The applied and often *implied* logic characterized by the words "if" and "how much more" is the modified analogy. The recognition of an analogy in the text depends completely on the experience of the reader. So, the use of words "how much more" may be *explicit or implicit*. The rule itself is defined as "from A follows B." It serves as an illustration in an argument and may be used to verify its validity. When somebody presumes the case of *kal vachomer* in a text, then one should take into account the goal of the presumed analogy. The right part of the analogy, which is the goal of the argument, is the most important part. The left part, which serves to illustrate, is the supporting part, and so it can often be replaced by any similar illustration.

If - illustration (left part), *how much more* - purpose (right part).

Now let's analyze some examples how the explicit and implicit rule *kal vachomer* is applied in the Bible (Prov. 11:31, 11, respectively):

> [31] *If* the righteous receive their due on earth, *how much more* the ungodly and the sinner!
> [11] By the blessing of the upright a city is exalted, but by the mouth of the wicked it is destroyed.

Verse 31 serves as a reference for understanding all other verses in chapters 10 and 11.

The goal of that argument is the right part: "the ungodly and the sinner will receive their due." We find the illustration and the base for the right part in "the righteous receive their due."

The knowledge of the rule assists in understanding the text.

The text about the Holy Spirit exemplifies the explicit rule (Luke 11:11-13):

> [11] And which of you fathers, if your son asks for a fish, will give him a snake instead? [12] Or if he asks for an egg, will give him a scorpion? [13] If you then, though you are evil, know how to give good gifts to your children, *how much more* will your Father in heaven give the Holy Spirit to those who ask him?"

The last part of the thirteenth verse amounts to the goal of the argument,[10] and the entire first part of the analogy is an illustration of the correctness of the second part. The first part may be easily changed to a similar one.

See also the text about riches for the world (Rom. 11:11-12):

> [11] And I ask: did they stumble so as to fall? Not at all! Rather, because of their transgression, salvation has come to the Gentiles to make them [Jews] envious. [12] But if their [Jews] transgression means riches for the world, and their loss means riches for the Gentiles, how big will be their fullness.

In this case the *kal vachomer* is *implicit*: if words could be changed slightly in the last sentence, then the following would be achieved: "*how much more* would be their fullness." This translation was done in NASB and ESB Bibles. In this example, the text of the proof is vital for the proof's objective.

The Sermon on the Mount has been analyzed and explained from many angles, so let us attempt to apply *kal vachomer* (Matt. 5:1-11):

> [1] And he saw the crowd, he went up on a mountainside and sat down. His disciples came to him, [2] and opening His mouth he began to teach them, saying: [3] blessed are the poor in spirit, for theirs is the kingdom of heaven. [4] Blessed are those who mourn, for they will be comforted. [5] Blessed are the meek, for they will inherit the earth. [6] Blessed are those who hunger and thirst for righteousness, for they will be filled. [7] Blessed are the merciful, for they will be shown mercy. [8] Blessed are the pure in heart, for they will see God. [9] Blessed are the peacemakers, for they will be called sons of God. [10] Blessed are those who are persecuted because of righteousness, for theirs is the kingdom of heaven.[11] Blessed are you when people insult you, persecute you and falsely say all kinds of evil against you because of me.

Matthew creates a picture that recalls the image of Moses after receiving the Ten Commandments.

---

10 Craig S. Keener, The IVP Bible background commentary: New Testament (1993) 219.

"Opening one's mouth . . , saying" in Matt. 5:2 is an idiom in Hebrew found in Job 3:1, Dan. 10:16. Matthew uses this expression in Matt. 13:35, and Luke uses it more often in Acts 8:34, 10:34, 18:14.

The third verse (Matt. 5:3) is based on Ps. 37:9, 11. Blessed, *ashre* in Hebrew, means associated with happiness and righteousness, as in Ps. 1:1. The poor in spirit are the *shaphal ruah*, those who are aware that they cannot receive salvation on their own terms, those in whom is the least of human pride (Prov. 16:19).

And if the believers of the past belong to the Kingdom of Heaven, *how much more* do those who believe today.

For Matt. 5:4, if God will comfort those who mourn; see Isa. 61:1-3, then *how much more* will He comfort those who believe in Him now.

For Matt. 5:5, meek is *anaw* in Hebrew; see Ps. 37:11, where this stands for gentle, humble, meek, poor, and peaceful. If they inherited the earth, then *how much more* will it happen to believers nowadays.

For Matt. 5:6, if God satisfies those who hunger for righteousness; see Isa. 55:1, then *how much more* will He satisfy believers today.

For Matt. 5:7, grace is *khesed* in Hebrew; see Prov. 11:17, where it is used in the context or mercy, the undeserved manifestation of love. If God had mercy with believers in Biblical times, then *how much more* this would happen to believers today, as believers encounter many more temptations today.

For Matt. 5:8, a pure heart has ritually pure thoughts, i.e., directed to God, a pure heart has ritually pure thoughts, i.e., directed to God; see Ps. 24:3-4, 6. If God promised that believers would see Him in the future, then *how much more* believers should seek Him with pure heart nowadays.

For Matt. 5:9, this refers to peace among people and with God; see Matt. 5:44-48. It is impossible to speak the Hebrew language without mentioning God. For example, "welcome" is *baruch haba*, "blessed is the coming one." If peacemakers are called sons of God, then *how much more* those who are believers in Jesus.

For Matt. 5:10-11, if anybody did not get in trouble because of their faith, they obviously posed no threat to Satan, and if they did, then *how much more* they deserve to enter the Kingdom of Heaven.

If people denigrated, persecuted, and lied about Jesus' disciples (1 Peter 4:14), then *how much more* harm would his disciples endure today. Easy life is not promised to believers. Not everyone who claims that he is a believer is truly a believer, especially if they persecute others.

Here is Paul's common way of reasoning (Rom. 11:16):

> [16] And if the part offered as first fruits is holy, then the whole batch is holy; and if the root is holy, and so are the branches.

A slight addition to the phrase makes the *kal vachomer explicit*:

> [16] And if the part offered as first fruits is holy, *how much more* the whole batch is holy; and if the root is holy, *how much more* are the branches.

In this verse Paul reasons that Jewish believers are sanctified.

Another example of implicit *kal vachomer* can be found in Rom. 8:9:

> [9] And you are not in the flesh but in the Spirit, if the Spirit of God dwells in you. And if anyone does not have the Spirit of Christ, he does not belong to Him.

The following verse could be changed to the explicit rule:

> [9] And if the Spirit of God dwells in you *how much more* you are not in the flesh. And if anyone does not have the Spirit of Christ, *how much less* he does not belong to Him.

The implicit parable is included into the Sermon on the Mount (Matt. 5:13):

> [13] "You are the salt of the earth. But if the salt becomes *foolish*, how can it be salty again? It is no longer effective for anything, except to be thrown out and trampled by [the feet of] men.

Salt was produced in ancient times by the evaporation of seawater, or by mining rock salt, the same way that it is produced today. Thus, salt cannot lose its saltiness.

The original Greek text differs in two places from most translations. The word "foolish" in the parable means the state of unbelief in God. The expression "trampled by feet" in Middle Eastern culture means a complete loss of respect or value. So, the parable may be paraphrased this way:

> [13]...If a man becomes an unbeliever, *how much less* is the chance that he will become a believer again. He has no more value for God, and will be thrown out in total disrespect.

The measure of human life is in his own faith in God.

The proper application of the rule "kal vachomer" drastically changes the understanding of the text, Rom. 13:1-8:

> [13:1] Every soul must submit oneself to the governing authorities, for there is no authority except that which God has established. And the authorities that exist have been established by God. [2] Therefore, he who rebels against the authority is rebelling against what God has instituted, and those who do so will bring judgment on themselves. [3] And rulers hold no terror for those who do right, but for those who do evil. Do you want to be free from fear of the one in authority? Then do what is right and you will have praise. [4] And he is God's servant to do you good. And if you do wrong, be afraid, and he does not bear the sword for nothing. He is God's servant, and an agent of wrath to bring punishment on the wrongdoer. [5] Therefore, it is necessary to submit to the authorities, not only because of possible punishment but also because of conscience. [6] And this is also why you pay taxes, for the authorities are God's servants, and who give their full time to governing. [7] Give everyone what you owe him: If you owe taxes, pay taxes; if revenue, then revenue; if respect, then respect; if honor, then honor. [8] Let no debt remain outstanding, except the continuing debt to love one another, and he who loves his fellowman has fulfilled the Law.

Commonly, this text is understood as a call to obey authorities, but the verse in 13:8 refers to something else. In Romans, everything is precise and follows the subject from the first word to the last, and the letter itself is written to a Church community that is no longer obedient to the Gospel.

In the Roman Empire withholding taxes was a very serious crime. The non-payer's whole family could be enslaved or even receive the death penalty. Thus, it was not necessary to persuade anyone to pay taxes. At this time, Emperor Nero ruled the Roman Empire, and he was not going to be lenient to Christians over money. Besides, what does the Law of Moses have to do at all with Roman taxation?

But if there is an implicit *kal vachomer*, then it is evident that if they obey the secular authorities, then *how much more* must they obey the Church's authorities, including Paul himself. God's servant works for everyone's benefit. Moreover, acceptance and love of fellow Christians in the Church are considered to be the fulfillment of Mosaic Law. Nevertheless, this Church in Rome rejected not only the letter, but also Paul himself.

The *kal vachomer* rule may be found not only in the Bible, but also in Talmudic literature, where Jews use it quite often:

> Yossei the son of Yochanan of Jerusalem would say: Let your home be wide open, and let the poor be members of your household. And do not engage in excessive conversation with a woman. This is said even regarding one's own wife; *how much more* so regarding the wife of another.[11]

Kal Vachomer in Parables

All parables are built on the *kal vachomer* rule, even if they do not contain the words "how much more," and *all* parables could be *always* paraphrased to include these words. Basically, the Hebrew terms *mashal* and *nimshal*, fable and explanation, which correspond to the left and right parts, then become easily distinguishable.[12]

---

11 Pirkei Avot, Ethics of the Fathers, 1.5.

12 Michael Wyschogrod, Parable and story in Judaism and Christianity By Clemens Thoma (1989) 30-37.

See the parable about disciples and the teacher (Matt. 10:24-25):

> [24] A student is not above his teacher, and nor a servant above his master. [25] It is enough for the student to be like his teacher, and the servant like his master. If the head of the house has been called Beelzebub, *how much more* the members of his household!

The text could be compared to Luke 6:39-40, teaching that students receive their teacher's imprint, whether good or bad in this straightforward parable.

See also the parable on avoiding anxiety (Luke 12:22-24):

> [22] And Jesus said to his disciples: "Therefore I tell you, do not worry about your life, what you will eat; or about your body, what you will wear. [23] Life is more than food, and the body more than clothes. [24] Consider the ravens: They do not sow or reap, they have no storeroom or barn; and God feeds them, *how much more* valuable you are than birds!

Luke tells five parables with a similar message. The left part of the parables could be easily replaced by any similar illustration. The message could be rephrased this way:

> Do not worry about your life because *how much more* are you valuable for God, Who gives life.

There is one more parable on the same subject, Luke 12:27-28:

> [27] Consider how the lilies grow. They do not labor or spin. And I tell you, not even Solomon in all his splendor was dressed like one of these. [28] And if that is how God clothes the grass of the field, which is here today, and tomorrow is thrown into the fire, *how much more* will he clothe you, O you of little faith.

This echoes the theme of a parable earlier in that chapter (Luke 12:22-24).

The parable about the Kingdom of God is an example of how to paraphrase it to make the parable explicit (Mark 4:26-29):

> [26] And He said, "This is what the kingdom of God is like. A man

scatters seed on the ground. [27] And he sleeps at night, and gets up at day, and the seed sprouts and grows, though he does not know how. [28] And all by itself the soil produces grain: first the stalk, then the head, then the full kernel in the head. [29] And as soon as the grain is ripe, he puts the sickle to it, because the harvest has come.

It can be paraphrased with the inclusion of *how much more*:

A man scatters seed on the ground. And he sleeps at night, and gets up at day, and the seed sprouts and grows, though he does not know how. And all by itself the soil produces grain: first the stalk, then the head, then the full kernel in the head. And as soon as the grain is ripe, he puts the sickle to it, because the harvest has come. *How much more* the Kingdom of God grows.

Another example of how to paraphrase a parable to make it explicit (Matt. 7:24-27):

[24] And everyone who hears these words of mine and puts them into practice is like a wise man who built his house on the rock. [25] And the rain came down, and the streams rose, and the winds blew and beat against that house; and it did not fall, and it had its foundation on the rock. [26] And everyone who hears these words of mine and does not put them into practice is like a foolish man who built his house on sand. [27] And the rain came down, and the streams rose, and the winds blew and beat against that house, and it fell and great was its fall.

The following is the paraphrase of the parable:

And everyone who hears these words of mine and does not put them into practice is like a foolish man who built his house on sand. *How much more* like a wise man is he who hears these words of mine and puts them into practice, who built his house on the rock.

Kal Vachomer in Parables with Negative Examples

Another obstacle in understanding the text of the Bible is the use of the negative example in parables. It is a challenge to interpret how the negative example can lead to a positive conclusion in the case when Jesus brings up negative behavior as an example. Pursuing the goal to explain the parable's logic, some commentators come up with the "hidden" or even imaginative meaning.[13]

The reasoning is very simple: even if an unbeliever does or does not do that, then *how much more* should believers in God do the same.

See the parable about persistence in prayer (Luke 11:5-10):

> [5] And he said to them, if one of you has a friend, and he goes to him at midnight and says, 'Friend, lend me three loaves of bread, [6] because a friend of mine on a journey has come to me, and I have nothing to set before him.' [7] And the one inside answers saying: Don't bother me. The door is already locked, and my children are with me in bed. I can't get up and give you anything.' [8] I tell you, though he will not get up and give him the bread because he is his friend, yet because of the man's impudence he will get up and give him as much as he needs. [9] And I say to you: Ask and it will be given to you; seek and you will find; knock and the door will be opened to you. [10] And everyone who asks receives; and he who seeks finds; and to him who knocks, the door will be opened.

While many commentaries persist in finding a reason why it is necessary to give bread, and sometimes state that the friend already gave that bread,[14] this evades the fact that the "friend" indisputably did not want to help. The meaning of the parable is the following: if people give bread in good faith or are forced to do it, *how much more* should believers expect help from God.

---

13 Edwin Wilbur Rice, People's commentary on the Gospel according to Luke (1889) 172; Joel B. Green, The Gospel of Luke (1997) 448.

14 An excellent example of an attempt to find a positive element where it does not exist, based on disregarding numerous pieces of evidence and changing the generally accepted meaning of the word to the opposite, can be found in Alan Johnson, "The Fallacy of Translating Anaideia by 'Persistence' in Luke 11:5-8," *Journal of the Evangelical Theological Society* 22 (1979) 121-131.

See the parable about the persistent widow (Luke 18:1-7):

> [1] And Jesus told his disciples a parable to show them that they should always pray and not give up. [2] He said: In a certain town there was a judge who not feared God and not cared about men. [3] And there was a widow in that town and she kept coming to him with the plea, Grant me protection from my opponent. [4] For some time he refused. But finally he said to himself, and though I don't fear God and don't care about men, [5] and because this widow keeps bothering me, I will see that she gets justice, so that she won't eventually wear me out with her coming! [6] And the Lord said, Listen to what the unjust judge says. [7] And will not God bring about justice for his chosen ones, who cry out to him day and night and will He delay long over them?

If even the unjust judge responds to requests, then *how much more* God cares for His righteous people. [15]

The parable about the thief and the strong owner of the house (Matt. 12:28-29):

> [28] And if I drive out demons by the Spirit of God, then the kingdom of God has come upon you. [29] Or again, how can anyone enter a strong man's house and carry off his possessions unless he first ties up the strong man? And only then he can rob his house.

Usually, the commentaries sensibly avoid the words about the robbery or stealing other man's possessions, especially if said by Jesus. The message is clear: if it is impossible to defeat all individual demons without the initial victory over Satan, then *how much more* is it easier when Jesus has already expelled demons, and the Kingdom of God is with us.

See the parable about the Kingdom of Heaven (Matt. 13:44):

> [44] The kingdom of heaven is like treasure hidden in a field. When a man found it, he hid it again, and then in his joy went and sold all he had and bought that field.

---

15 Craig S. Keener, The IVP Bible background commentary: New Testament (1993) 238.

In this parable, the buyer defrauds the owner of the land by doing what is condemned by the Law of Moses, and breaking the following commandments:

Do not be dishonest — Lev. 19:35
Return found or lost property to the owner — Deut. 22:1
Do not lie about property's ownership — Lev. 19:11
Do not steal — Lev. 19:11
Do not desire other man property — Deut. 5:21

If people are ready to do anything for the sake of personal wealth, then *how much more* should they desire such a fortune as the Kingdom of Heaven.

See the parable about the dishonest manager (Luke 16:1-10):

> [1] And he said to his disciples, there was a rich man who had a manager, and charges were brought to him that this man was wasting his possessions. [2] And he called him and said to him, what is this that I hear about you? Turn in the account of your management, and you can no longer be manager. [3] And the manager said to himself, what shall I do, since my master is taking the management away from me? I am not strong enough to dig, and I am ashamed to beg. [4] I have decided what to do, so that when I am removed from management, people may receive me into their houses. [5] And summoning his master's debtors one by one, he said to the first, how much do you owe my master? [6] He said, A hundred bat of oil. He said to him, Take your bill, and sit down quickly and write fifty. [7] Then he said to another, and how much do you owe? He said, A hundred kor of wheat. He said to him, Take your bill, and write eighty. [8] And the master commended the dishonest manager for his shrewdness. For the sons of this age are more shrewd in dealing with their own generation than the sons of light. [9] And I tell you, make friends for yourselves by means of unrighteous wealth, so that when you fail they may receive you into the eternal dwellings. [10] Whoever can be trusted with very little can also be trusted with much, and whoever is dishonest with very little will also be dishonest with much.

It is truly hard without the application of Semitic logic to understand whether Jesus recommends emulating the behavior of the dishonest manager. Thus, some commentaries state that Jesus simply could not give a negative example, and therefore it is necessary to find something positive in the manager who embezzled the money.[16] And when the manager was unsuccessful, his master, himself a criminal, found the crime and made the manager a co-conspirator.

In truth, it's much simpler: if a dishonest manager cared about his own future, than *how much more* should one take care of one's own eternal soul. If the deceitful master praised the dishonest manager, then *how much more* will God praise His own truthful believers.

Gezera Shava

The *gezera shava* is another kind of Semitic logic which is even more challenging than *kal vachomer* and also unfamiliar to most believers. The rule is sometimes applied to two texts, descriptions, or events that are considered to be in agreement if they *have at least one common word*. Preferably, it should be a key word offering the analogy. The repetition of a specific term in another context is an indication for a possibility of a comparison. In European/ Western reasoning, analogies are built on a much more stringent connection. Naturally, it is necessary to identify this word and define the intent of the author. After all, there should be some restrictions in the use of *gezera shava*.

It is obvious that the identification of *gezera shava* is very subjective. The readers who are unfamiliar with the rule or are unable to find it in a text may become very frustrated when they fail to understand the logic of some verses of the New Testament.

One can find a perfect example in Matt. 2:17-18:

> [17] Then what was said through the prophet Jeremiah was fulfilled: [18] A voice is heard in Ramah, *weeping* and great mourning, Rachel weeping for her children and refusing to be comforted, because they are no more.

The quotation is taken from Jer. 31:15, but it must be understood in the

---

16 An example of that logic may be found in Thomas L. Constable, Notes on Luke (2010) 186.

context of Jer. 31:1, 15-17:

> [1] At that time, declares the Lord, I will be the God of all the clans of Israel, and they will be my people...
> [15] This is what the Lord says: A voice is heard in Ramah, mourning and great *weeping*, Rachel weeping for her children and refusing to be comforted, because her children are no more. [16] This is what the Lord says: Restrain your voice from weeping and your eyes from tears, for your work will be rewarded, declares the Lord. And they will return from the land of the enemy. [17] So there is hope for your future, declares the Lord, and your children will return to their own land.

Rachel is the name of the city of the Northern Kingdom which was destroyed in 722 B.C. Using *gezera shava*, Jeremiah mourns the Southern Kingdom, which perished in 586 B.C. Matthew adds his own events, comparing all the events that took place in different cities with different people and at different times, also applying *gezera shava*. In the application of this rule, the common word is "weeping," and the goal of the rule would be accomplished by Jesus who comforts those who are in grief, and corrects everything that is wrong.

Jeremiah makes use of *gezera shava* in his text, and in his turn, Matthew applies the same rule to the text of Jeremiah. Such a chain in Semitic logic might be considerably longer.

Jesus cleanses the Temple (Mark 11:15-17):

> [15] And on reaching Jerusalem, Jesus entered the Temple and began driving out those who were buying and selling in the Temple. And he overturned the tables of the money changers and the benches of those selling doves, [16] and would not allow anyone to carry merchandise through the Temple. [17] And as he taught them, and he said, Is it not written: My house will be called a house of prayer for all Gentiles? And you have made it a *cave of robbers*.

The quotes are given from the LXX (Isa. 56:7, Jer. 7:11), but it is a challenge to understand from Mark's text how Jesus put together the quotations from both prophets.[17] A quick look at the context reveals how the words "My house" explain the presence of *gezera shava* in the text (Isa. 56:7):

> [7] these I will bring to my holy mountain and give them joy in *my house* of prayer. Their burnt offerings and sacrifices will be accepted on my altar; and *my house* will be called a house of prayer for all Gentiles.

Jer. 7:11:

> [11] Has *my house*, which bears my Name, become a cave of robbers to you? And I have seen it, declares the Lord.

The Semitic logic of reasoning in the New Testament is not always obvious. Peter in Acts 2:25-36 shows that Jesus is the Messiah and God by drawing an analogy between the events of King David's life and the prophecies:

> [25] And David said about him: I saw the Lord always before me, because he is *at my right hand*, that I will not be shaken. [26] Therefore my heart is glad and my tongue rejoices; and my body also will live in hope, [27] because you will not abandon me to Hades, and will not you let your Holy One see decay. [28] You have made known to me the paths of life; you will fill me with joy in your presence. [29] Brothers, I can tell you confidently that the patriarch David and died, and was buried, and his tomb is here to this day. [30] And he was a prophet and knew that God had promised him on oath that he would place one of the fruit of his loins on his throne. [31] Seeing what was ahead, he spoke of the resurrection of the Christ, that he was not abandoned to the Hades, nor did his body see decay. [32] God has raised this Jesus to life, and we are all witnesses of the fact. [33] And exalted to the *right hand* of God, and he has received from the Father the promised Holy Spirit and has poured out what you now see and hear. [34] And David did not ascend to heaven, and yet he said, The Lord said to my Lord: Sit *at my right hand* [35] until I make your enemies a footstool for your feet. [36] And let all house of Israel

---

17 Bruce Chilton, Craig A. Evans, Studying the historical Jesus: evaluations of the state of current research (1998) 288-290.

be assured of this: God has made this Jesus, whom you crucified, both Lord and Christ."

Peter quotes Ps. 16:8-11 and Ps. 110:1, written at different times and on different occasions, linking them together with *gezera shava* (Ps. 16:8-11):

> [8] I have set the Lord always before me. Because he is at *my right hand*, I will not be shaken. [9] Therefore my heart is glad and my tongue rejoices; my body also will rest secure, [10] because you will not abandon me to the Sheol, nor will you let your Holy One see decay. [11] You have made known to me the path of life; you will fill me with joy in your presence, with eternal pleasures at your *right hand*.

Ps. 110:1:

> [1] The Lord says to my Lord: Sit at *my right hand* until I make your enemies a footstool for your feet.

The key words in both psalms are "at my right hand," which make it possible for Peter to connect them.

Let us see how *gezera shava* is applied to the text in Matt. 3:1-4:

> [1] And in those days John the Baptist came, preaching in the Desert of Judea [2] and saying, "Repent, and the kingdom of heaven is near." [3] And this is he who was spoken of through the prophet Isaiah saying: "A voice of one calling in the desert, Prepare the way for the Lord, make straight paths for him." [4] And John's clothes were made of camel's hair, and he had a leather belt around his waist. And his food was locusts and wild honey.

To carry out baptisms in a desert may seem impossible for those who are unfamiliar with the geography of Israel. The Jordan River flows through the Jordan Valley, often changing its course and constantly turning. On both sides of the river, trees and shrubs grow, stretching up to three hundred feet from the shore, at the edge of which the vegetation suddenly ends and the beige limestone desert starts. Though he baptized in the water, John did live in the wilderness of Jordan valley, where the shallow river can be easily overlooked from the outside.

There were hardly any locusts and bees in the desert; in all likelihood John had to eat common food. Matthew portrays the image of a prophet who speaks the word of God and is independent from other people. John depended on God only.

The image of John in camel's hair and leather belt immediately brings to mind the prophet Elijah. The *gezera shava* rule leads to the comparison of John and Elijah in 2 Kings 1:8:

> [8]...He was a man with a garment of hair and with a leather belt around his waist...

The quotation in Matt. 3:3 is given from the LXX version of Isa. 40:3, but it is better to read it in the context of Isa. 40:1-5, where it is written that the Glory of God will be revealed:

> [1] Comfort, comfort my people, says your God. [2] Speak tenderly to Jerusalem, and proclaim to her that her warfare has been completed, that her iniquity has been removed, that she has received from the Lord's hand double for all her sins. [3] A voice of one calling: In the desert prepare the way for the Lord; make straight in the wilderness a highway for our God. [4] Every valley shall be raised up, and every mountain and hill made low; and the rough ground shall become level, and the rugged places a plain. [5] And the glory of the Lord will be revealed, and all flesh together will see it. For the mouth of the Lord has spoken.

According to *gezera shava*, the desert is the common word as well in Isa. 40:3:

> [3] A voice of one calling: In the desert prepare the way...

See also John 1:23:

> [23] John said, "I am the voice of one calling in the desert, make straight the way for the Lord," as Isaiah the prophet said.

Both John the Baptist and the Apostle John knew how to use *gezera shava*.

Analogy

Analogy in the Bible may transform the story by adding a new meaning which has been hidden or which was not obvious at first glance. Paul used this literary device in Gal. 4:21-31. Often it is used to entertain others with a very elaborate analogy. Great benefit can be reaped from understanding how Paul frequently practiced Semitic logic. Since the time of the apostles, there have been constant attempts to recreate Paul's logic without understanding his goal and skills. Semitic logic is straightforward; analogies are built together to gradually turn the original statement into the final statement. This is done by multiple uses of *gezera shava*, and the process is remarkably similar to the game of transforming one word into another and creating a word ladder, when only one letter is changed each time. For example:

cold → cord → card → ward → warm

It is always important to discern the author's intention, as building analogies is quite subjective.

Paul's analogy serves as an example. His first step can be found in Gal. 4:21-23:

> 21 Tell me, you who want to be under the Law, are you not aware of what the Law says? 22 And it is written that Abraham had two sons, one by the slave woman and the other by the free woman. 23 His son by the slave was born according to the flesh; but his son by the free woman was born as the result of a promise.

Since Paul chose the dual themes of slavery and freedom, and the main theme is God's promise of Isaac's birth, then Gentile Christians (and this is a secondary theme) were also born in Jesus by promise. That is the way that *gezera shava* connects the Law and slavery.

The second step (Gal. 4:24):

> 24 These things *are figurative*, and the women represent two covenants. One covenant is from Mount Sinai and bears children who are to be slaves: This is Hagar.

Slavery is the primary theme by which Paul associates Hagar and the

Old Testament.

The third step (Gal. 4:25):

> [25] And Hagar stands for Mount Sinai in Arabia and corresponds to the present city of Jerusalem, and she is in slavery with her children.

Because the Old Testament binds together Mount Sinai and Jews, and the Temple Mount binds together Jews and Jerusalem, Jerusalem is in bondage just like Hagar. The logic already seems to be whimsical.

The fourth step (Gal. 4:26):

> [26] And the Jerusalem that is above [heavenly] is free, and she is our mother.

As both Sarah and heavenly Jerusalem are free, Jerusalem becomes the ancestors' place of believers.

The fifth step (Gal. 4:27-28):

> [27] And it is written: Be glad, O barren woman, who bears no children; break forth and cry aloud, you who have no labor pains; because more are the children of the desolate woman than of her who has a husband. [28] And you, brothers, like Isaac, are children of promise.

Because *all* believers are descendants of Abraham and Sarah, all the promises made to Jews also apply to Gentile believers, even though Isaiah wrote about Israel during the time of Babylonian captivity and did not mention Gentiles.

The sixth step (Gal 4:29):

> [29] At that time the son born in flesh persecuted the son born in Spirit. And it is the same now.

Because Ishmael is identified with unbelieving Jews, the relationship between Ishmael and Isaac can be transferred to the relationship of the Jerusalem Church with unbelieving Jews. The persecution of the Church in Jerusalem is the reference here.

The seventh step (Gal. 4:30):

> [30] But what does the Scripture say? Get rid of the slave woman and her son, for the slave's son will never share in the inheritance with the free woman's son.

Because Hagar in Abraham's house is identified with unbelievers within the Church, Sarah's proposed solution to her problem can be viewed as the solution to the problem in the Galatian Churches. This means that there can be no possible union of Christian believers and unbelieving Church leaders. All of this was overlaid with the image of Paul's opponents in the Galatian Churches: the former idolaters, who retained some of their old habits, added observance of Judaism which they misunderstood, and tried to blend all of this with their faith in Jesus.

The eighth step (Gal. 4:31):

> [31] Therefore, brothers, we are not children of the slave, but of the free woman.

Because Gentile Christians are no longer identified with unbelievers, they are counted among the descendants of Israel. Paul will develop this idea further in Romans 11.

Thus, we have seen that Paul consecutively applies *gezera shava* eight times. It is obvious that Paul's arguments are always oriented toward people who already know the fundamentals of Judaism and understand the Semitic way of reasoning. Naturally, the question arises: could Galatians, who were Christians for about two years or less, understand such complex Semitic logic? Therefore, in spite of the fact that he wrote his letter to a mostly Gentile audience, Paul needed a group of Jews within the Church to explain his letter to Gentiles. Unfortunately, the existence of such a group is unlikely in today's Church.

As a result, non-Biblical explanations of this text found their way to many Churches, and could be used successfully by the enemies of both Paul and Jesus to condemn them. There is no need to seek out false witnesses or falsify the facts, because misinformed Christians will do it for them.

Typology, Allegory, and sensus plenior

With a knowledge of Semitic logic, there is no need for a theologian to come up with new methods or theories such as typology, allegory, or *sensus plenior*.

Typology is a doctrine regarding how the Old Testament relates to the New Testament, where events, persons, or statements in the Old Testament are seen as types superseded by antitypes of events, or Christ's descriptions, or His revelations in the New Testament. In the fullest version of the typology, the whole purpose of the Old Testament is viewed merely as the shadow of types for fulfillment in Christ and in the New Testament.

But typology cannot explain *all* uses of Semitic logic, and thus allegory is then added to explain the misunderstood text using a new, "spiritual" meaning. Usually, such typological and allegorical readings are pure pseudo-theological fantasies.

Allegory fails short likewise, and consequently, the *sensus plenior* approach was invented. This method is supposed to find a deeper meaning not intended by the original authors, which is nonetheless clear to a modern commentator. One only needs to "discover" what the text *should* mean, disregarding the author's intention and thought.

Midrash

In the twenty-first century some commentators started to include Midrash, the rabbinic method of interpreting the Bible, and other rabbinic teaching, including the Talmud, which assumes that words, letters, numbers, and ideas represent something that is being not openly stated in the text, i.e., a hidden meaning. Through the Midrashic process, rabbis try to make Judaism relevant to their contemporaries, to teach moral lessons, and to tell elaborate stories with a hint of the unreal. Through this approach of studying the New Testament, Midrash becomes intertwined with typology, allegory, *sensus plenior*, and the imagination.[18]

---

18 Kenneth Berding and Jonathan Lunde, A failure to understand Semitic logic may be discerned from Three Views on the New Testament Use of the Old Testament (2008).

Covenants

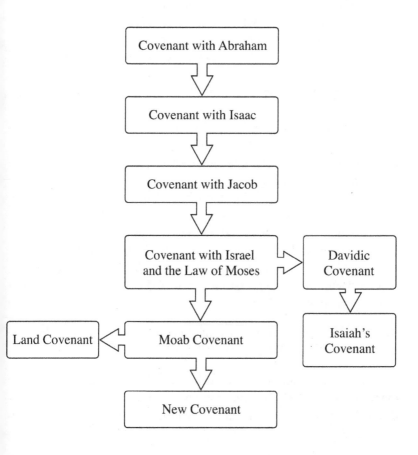

Covenants with Israel

Covenant with Abraham

The covenant with Abraham is based on six Biblical passages: Gen. 12:1-3, 7, 13:14-17, 15:1-21, 17:1-21, 22:15-18. God established through the Covenant the following:

- The great nation will come from Abraham: the people of Israel (Gen. 12:2, 13:16, 15:5, 17:1-2, 7, 22:17).
- The land of Israel is bequeathed to Abraham (Gen. 12:1, 7, 13:14-15, 17, 15:17-21, 17:8).
- Abraham is blessed by God (Gen. 12:2, 15:6, 22:15-17).
- Abraham's name will be great (Gen. 12:2).
- Abraham will be a blessing to others (Gen. 12:2).
- Through Abraham Gentiles will be blessed (Gen. 22:18).
- Sarah will have a son born to Abraham (Gen. 15:1-4, 17:16-21).
- Abraham's descendants will be oppressed in Egypt (Gen. 15:13-14).
- His name will be changed from *Avram* to *Avraham*.[19] Avraham means "a father of many nations," as from Abraham will come not only Israel, but also other nations, including the Arab nations (Gen. 17:3-6).
- His wife's name will be changed from Sarai to Sarah (Gen. 17:15). In Hebrew, the last letter "yod" is changed to "hey," which is not pronounced (both mean "princess").
- Circumcision is given as a token of the Covenant (Gen. 17:9-14); as a commandment it will be included in the Law of Moses.
- "I will bless them that bless you and curse him that dishonor you" (Gen. 12:3).

The implementation of the Covenant begins in Gen. 12:1, *before* the statements in Gen. 17:1-2, 22:16-18, 26:3-5.

The Land Covenant is one-sided because God was alone when He made it (Gen. 15:8-18); consequently, the Land Covenant is unconditional, and the unconditional Covenant cannot be part of the conditional one.

The Covenant with Abraham remained valid after the events in Gen.

---

19 *Avraham,* אַבְרָהָם, is Hebrew pronunciation.

12:13, 16, and 20:2. Abraham had sinned, but God confirmed the Covenant (Gen. 26:1-4). When Isaac had sinned (Gen. 26:6-11), God confirmed the Covenant with Jacob (Gen. 28:13-15, 35:9-12, 48:3-4). When the sons of Jacob had sinned (Gen. 37:18-36, 38:12-26), Joseph (Gen. 50:24-26) believed that the Covenant was still valid. Much later, God told Moses in Ex. 2:24, 6:2-8 that the Covenant with Abraham was still in effect. Moses stated that even after the punishment for sins, God would remain faithful to the Covenant with Abraham (Deut. 4:25-31). King David believed that the Covenant with Abraham was still valid (1 Chron. 16:15-18 and Ps. 105:8-11).

In Luke 1:67-75 the same acceptance of the Covenant's legitimacy is described as a prophecy:

> [67] And his father Zechariah was filled with the Holy Spirit and prophesied, saying: [68] Praise be to the Lord, the God of Israel, because he has come and has redeemed his people. [69] He has raised up a horn of salvation for us in the house of his servant David [70] as he said by the mouth of his holy prophets of old, [71] salvation from our enemies and from the hand of all who hate us [72] to show mercy to our fathers and to remember his holy covenant, [73] the oath he swore to our father Abraham to grant us [74] that we, being delivered from the hand of our enemies, might serve him without fear [75] in holiness and righteousness before him all our days of life.

In Acts 3:25-26, Peter announced in the Temple that the Covenant with Abraham had been fulfilled in Jesus:

> [25] It is you who are the sons of the prophets and of the covenant God made with our fathers, saying to Abraham: And in your off-spring all families on earth will be blessed. [26] When God raised up his servant Jesus, he sent him first to you to bless you by turning each of you from your wicked ways.

In Heb. 6:13-18 God shows the immutability of His Covenant:

> [13] When God made his promise to Abraham, since there was no one greater for him to swear by, he swore by himself, [14] saying, I will with blessings bless you and multiplying multiply you. [15] And so after waiting patiently, Abraham obtained the promise. [16] And

men swear by someone greater than themselves, and the oath confirms the end to all argument. [17] Because God wanted to make the unchanging nature of his purpose to the heirs of what was promised, he confirmed it with an oath. [18] And by two unchangeable things in which it is impossible for God to lie, we who have fled to take hold of the hope offered to us may be greatly encouraged.

It is very important to note that when the Letter to Hebrews was composed (in 69-70 A.D.), most of Israel had not accepted Jesus as the Messiah. Nevertheless, the Covenant with Abraham *continued to be in force*. Moreover, it also *encompassed* Gentile Christians.

Covenants with Isaac and Jacob

God reiterated the Abrahamic Covenant with his descendants (Gen. 26:2-6, 24, 28:12-15, 35:9-12), specifying that the Messianic line would go through Isaac rather than Ishmael (and later with Jacob, rather than Esau). God's promise is everlasting.

Land Covenant

Usually, believers do not separate the Land Covenant and the Abrahamic Covenant as God *promised* the land to Abraham initially (Gen. 12:1, 7-8, 15:18). However, the Land Covenant was established as a distinct agreement with Israel (Deut. 29:10-15, 29:22-30:10, 32:49), where the Lord *had given* the land. This is a separate Covenant, as can be seen from Deut. 29:1.

The Lord's oath, which is mentioned thirty five times in the Old Testament, has cemented the Covenant: see Ex. 6:8, 13:5, 11; 33:1; Num. 14:23, 30; 32:11; Deut. 1:8, 35; 6:10, 18; 7:13; 8:1; 9:5; 10:11; 11:9, 21; 16:3, 15; 26:3, 15; 28:11; 30:20; 31:20-21, 23; 34: 4; Josh. 1:6, 14:9; Neh. 9:15; Jer. 11:5; 32:22; Ezek. 20:6, 15, 28; 47:14. The Land Covenant places an emphasis on a future for Israel in the Promised Land.

From now on, the fate of Israel and of the land are intertwined. The ownership of the land is directly dependent on the faith of Israel. Being judged by God, Israel is driven out from the land, and the blessing of Israel's faith is in her coming back to the Promised Land.

For a long time, the Church considered the Land Covenant to be a conditional Covenant. The small number of Jews in the land of Israel was used as evidence, i.e., the Church taught that the punishment was permanent, and repentance was blatantly declared nonexistent. The reexamination of this error began with theology of dispensations only in the nineteenth century, which affirmed the unconditional nature of the Land Covenant. There is some logic in this: the conditional nature of the Land Covenant entails the conditional nature of all other Covenants with Israel, which contradicts the interpretation of the prophecies by this particular theological approach.

But those contradictions would never arise, if the Church paid attention to words of Moses in Deut. 30:1-10:

> [1] And when all these words come upon you, blessing and curse, which I have set before you and you take them to mind among all the Gentiles where the Lord your God disperses you, [2] and when return to the Lord your God, you and your children, and obey him with all your heart and with all your soul according to everything I command you today, [3] then the Lord your God will bring you back from captivity and have compassion on you and gather you again from all the nations where he scattered you. [4] Even if you have been banished to the most distant land under the heavens, from there the Lord your God will gather you and bring you back. [5] And the Lord your God will bring you to the land that belonged to your fathers, and you will possess it, and he will prosper you, and he will make you more numerous than your fathers. [6] The Lord your God will circumcise your heart and the heart of your descendants, so that you may love him with all your heart and with all your soul, and you may live. [7] And the Lord your God will put all these curses on your enemies, and on those who hate, who persecute you. [8] And you will again listen to the voice of the Lord and follow all his commands I am giving you today. [9] And the Lord your God will prosper you abundantly in all the work of your hands, in the fruit of your womb, and the young of your livestock, and the crops of your land. The Lord will again rejoice in you and make you pros-

perous, just as he rejoiced in your fathers, [10] if you listen to the voice of the Lord your God and keep his commands and decrees that are written in this Book of the Law and turn to the Lord your God with all your heart and with all your soul.

It is clear from the text that the Land Covenant is unconditional, but rewards and punishments are conditional, as they depend on faith or disbelief.

The Bible presents the Covenant as *everlasting* after the return from the Babylonian captivity in 1 Chron. 16:15-18:

> [15] Remember his Covenant *forever*, the word he commanded, for a thousand generations, [16] the Covenant he made with Abraham, and the oath he swore to Isaac. [17] And He confirmed it to Jacob as a law, and to Israel as an *everlasting* Covenant, [18] saying: to you I will give the land of Canaan as the portion you will inherit.

Ps. 105:8-11 differs from 1 Chron. 16:15-18 only in the statement that God promises to remember His Covenant *forever*, rather than that Israel would remember the Covenant:

> [8] *He remembers* his Covenant *forever*, the promise he ordained for a thousand generations—[9] the Covenant he made with Abraham, swore to Isaac, [10] and confirmed to Jacob as a decree and to Israel as a permanent covenant: [11] "I will give the land of Canaan to you as your inherited portion."

All misinterpretations were resolved with the establishment of the nation-state of Israel in 1948, where it became clear that the Land Covenant is *forever* remembered by both God and Israel.

Isaiah prophesied that the land's inheritance is forever (Isa. 60:21):

> [21] And then will all your people be righteous and they will possess the land forever. They are the shoot I have planted, the work of my hands, for the display of my splendor.

Jeremiah wrote that Gentile believers will join Israel in Jerusalem (Jer. 3:15-19):

¹⁵ And I will give you shepherds after my own heart, who will lead you with knowledge and understanding. ¹⁶ And it shall come to pass, when you have multiplied and been fruitful in the land," declares the Lord, "men will no longer say, 'The ark of the covenant of the Lord.' It will never enter their mind and not be remembered, it will not be missed, and another one will not be made. ¹⁷ At that time they will call Jerusalem the Throne of the Lord, and all Gentiles will gather in Jerusalem to honor the name of the Lord, and no longer will they walk after the stubbornness of their evil heart. ¹⁸ In those days the house of Judah will walk with the house of Israel, and together they will come from a northern land to the land I gave your forefathers as an inheritance. ¹⁹ And I myself said, how gladly would set you among my sons and give you a desirable land, the most beautiful inheritance of all Gentiles. And I thought you would call me My Father and not turn away from me.

We may conclude the following:

- God will bring Israel back to her land, which was given *forever*;
- He will not do it because Israel is righteous, but because of His promise made to the forefathers;
- not only Jews will be gathered in Jerusalem, but also Gentile believers.

Everlasting possession of the land implies the *everlasting* existence of Israel; regardless of the conditional part, God keeps His promises.

Davidic Covenant

This Covenant is unique as it is always considered everlasting and unconditional without taking into account King David's sins, which included envy, deceit, murder, and adultery. The Messiah Jesus was promised in the Covenant, and God's steadfast love did not depart from David as it did from Saul.

The Covenant is given in two places recorded long after the death of King David, first in 2 Sam. 7:11-16:

¹¹ and have done ever since the time I appointed judges over my

people Israel, and I will also give you rest from all your enemies. The Lord declares to you that the Lord himself will establish a house for you. [12] When your days are over and you will sleep with your fathers, I will raise up your seed to succeed you, who will come from your own body, and I will establish his kingdom. [13] He is the one who will build a house for my Name, and I will establish the throne of his kingdom forever. [14] I will be his father, and he will be my son, and if he does wrong, I will punish him with the rod of men, with floggings inflicted by men. [15] And my love will never be taken away from him, as I took it away from Saul, whom I removed from before your face. [16] And your house and your kingdom will endure forever before my face, your throne will be established forever.

The Kingdom of David (and Solomon as his successor) is established forever, and David's descendants will remain forever.

The same promise is found in 1 Chron. 17:10-15:

[10] and have done ever since the time I appointed judges over my people Israel, and I will also subdue all your enemies. I declare to you that the Lord will build a house for you. [11] When your days are over and you will sleep with your fathers, I will raise up your seed to succeed you, one of your sons, and I will establish his kingdom. [12] He is the one who will build a house for me, and I will establish his throne forever. [13] I will be his father, and he will be my son, and I will never take my love away from him, as I took it away from your predecessor. [14] And I will set him over my house and my kingdom forever, and his throne will be established forever.

Isaiah 11:1 describes the shoot that will come from the stump of Jesse, reminding the reader of 2 Sam. 7. The everlasting Kingdom will come from Jesse's son David through the Messiah Jesus.

It follows from both texts that:

- The Davidic Covenant is everlasting, unconditional, and imposes the punishment for sins
- It is connected with the Mosaic Covenant, which is also everlasting and unconditional

- The Davidic Covenant brings the coming of Messiah, David's descendant, and His Kingdom
- Most importantly, Messiah is forever.

Despite Solomon's conditional part of the Covenant, God remains faithful to His promises.

Covenant with Israel

Promise of the Covenant

From the fourth century the early Church began teaching that the Covenant with Israel was no longer valid, but all Messianic believers always insist that the Covenant is still in force.[20] According to Rom. 9:1-5 the Covenant is unaffected by the level of Israel's obedience or disobedience.

Many authors claim that all Covenants, except the Covenant with Israel, are based on the promise of God,[21] and conclude that the Covenant with Israel must be temporary. Pursuing the idea to exclude Israel from her inheritance, they by necessity disregard that the Covenant with Israel was *also promised*. See Ex. 6:6-8:

> [6] Therefore, say to the sons of Israel: I am the Lord, and I will bring you out from under the yoke of the Egyptians. I will free you from being slaves to them, and I will redeem you with an outstretched arm and with mighty acts of judgment. [7] I will take you as my own people, and I will be your God. And you will know that I am the Lord your God, who brought you out from under the yoke of the Egyptians. [8] And I will bring you to the land I swore with uplifted hand to give to Abraham, to Isaac and to Jacob, and I will give it to you as a possession. I am the Lord.

---

20 Darrell L. Bock, Mitchell Glaser, To the Jew First: The Case for Jewish Evangelism in Scripture and History (2008).

21 J. Dwight Pentecost, Thy Kingdom Come (1995) 85; Robert Saucy, The Case for Progressive Dispensationalism (2010) 121; Herbert W. Bateman, Stanley D. Toussaint, J. Lanier Burns, Three Central Issues in Contemporary Dispensationalism (1999) 85-86; Kim Riddlebarger, Case for Amillennialism, A: Understanding the End Times (2003) 46.

What God has promised to Israel is hard to overestimate:

- Fulfill the oath to Abraham, Isaac, and Jacob
- Redeem Israel from slavery
- Bring Jews out of Egypt and into the land of Israel
- Give the land of Israel into her possession
- Make Israel His people
- Remain the God of Israel

These verses are the promise of the First Commandment which is the foundation of the Law of Moses.

Purpose of the Covenant

Why do so many people today reason that the unconditional Davidic Covenant and the Land Covenant are not part of the conditional Covenant with Israel? What is the origin of the premise that the "right" Covenants are based on the "wrong" Covenant? Is it possible that God could make the "wrong" Covenant?

The Sinaitic Covenant is correctly called the Covenant with Israel, not the Covenant with Moses as Israel's spokesman, because Moses was merely a mediator between God and Israel (Ex. 34:27-28):

> [27] And the Lord said to Moses, "Write down these words, for in accordance with these words I have made a Covenant with you and with Israel." [28] And Moses was there with the Lord forty days and forty nights without eating bread and without drinking water. And he wrote on the tablets the words of the Covenant—the *Ten Words*.

Ex. 19:3-6:

> [3] Then Moses went up to God, and the Lord called to him from the mountain, saying: "This is what you are to say to the house of Jacob and what you are to tell the sons of Israel: [4] You yourselves have seen what I did to Egypt, and how I carried you on eagles' wings and brought you to myself. [5] And now if you obey me fully and keep my Covenant, then out of all Gentiles you will be my treasured possession. And the whole earth is mine, [6] and you will

be for me a kingdom of priests and a holy nation. These are the words you are to speak to the Israelites."

The purpose of the Covenant is defined in verse 6: *to be a holy people*, i.e., to be the people who are faithful to God.

The everlasting Covenant with Israel was later reaffirmed (Lev. 24:8-9):

> [8] Every Sabbath day Aaron shall arrange it before the Lord regularly, it is from the sons of Israel as a *Covenant forever*. [9] It belongs to Aaron and his sons, who are to eat it in a holy place, because it is a most holy part of their regular share of the offerings made to the Lord by fire, *portion forever*.

Num. 18:19:

> [19] Whatever is set aside from the holy offerings the sons of Israel present to the Lord I give to you and your sons and daughters as an *everlasting* due. It is an *everlasting* covenant of salt before the Lord for both you and your offspring.

The works of the Covenant with Israel do not bring salvation (Ex. 31:12-13, 17):

> [12] And the Lord said to Moses, [13] Say to the Israelites, You must observe my Sabbaths. This will be a sign between me and you for *all* generations to come, so you may know that I am the Lord, who makes you holy.
> [17] It will be a sign between me and the Israelites *forever*, for in six days the Lord made the heavens and the earth, and on the seventh day he abstained from work and rested.

Since the Mosaic Law pointed out sin, Israel received it as the provision for instruction in righteousness. The Law keeps them separated from the pagan world as God's holy people. Ex. 31:13 confirms the purpose of the Law expressed in Ex. 19:6.

The Covenant Is Everlasting

The only possible origin of the teaching on the temporary Covenant with Israel is the errant doctrine of supersessionism or Replacement Theology. It stipulates that the Church supersedes Israel because of Israel's rejection of Jesus, and God has chosen the Church *instead* of Israel. It rejects the teaching that the New Covenant has been made with Israel (Jer. 31:31-33).

Since the sign of the Covenant with Israel is the Sabbath, thus there are persistent attempts to declare the fourth commandment to be null and void.

In Hebrew, the Covenant with Israel (the Mosaic Covenant) is called the Torah, which means "teaching" in Hebrew. The Torah is comprised of the five books of Moses, or the Law; Christian scholars refer to these books as the Pentateuch. In the Jewish mind, the *Torah*, as part of the Old Testament, cannot exist without the Covenant with Israel, or without Jews.

The teaching that the Covenant with Israel starts with events described in Ex. 19:18 is erroneous. The five references to the Torah *before* Exodus and receiving the Law as follows Gen. 26:5:

> [5] Because Abraham obeyed me and *kept* my requirements, my commands, my decrees and my laws.

Ex. 12:49:

> [49] The one Law [Torah] shall be to the *native-born and to the alien* living among you.

Ex. 13:9:

> [9] And it [the statements about Matzo festival, Pesach, Passover] will be for you like a sign on your hand and a reminder on your forehead that the Law of the Lord is to be in your mouth. For the Lord brought you out of Egypt with his mighty hand.

Ex. 16:4:

> [4] And the Lord said to Moses, "I will rain down bread from heaven

for you. The people are to go out each day and gather enough for that day. In this way I will test them and see whether they will walk in my Law [Torah]."

Ex. 18:16:

> [16] Whenever they have a dispute, it is brought to me, and I decide between the parties and inform them of God's decrees and Laws.

These verses demonstrate that the Covenant with Israel and the Law are inseparably conflated, and the Covenants in the *Torah* stay within the context of the exodus from Egypt, the most significant event in Jewish history.

The existence of the Torah before the time that Moses received the tablets with Commandments is not surprising. Wisdom as the manifestation of the Word of God existed before the foundation of the world (Ps. 33:6):

> [6] By the word of the Lord were the heavens made, their starry host by the breath of His mouth.

In the Proverbs, Wisdom is identified as the Torah (Prov. 8:22-36):

> [22] "The Lord possessed me at the beginning of His way, before his deeds of old; [23] I was appointed from eternity, from the beginning, before the world began. [24] When there were no oceans, I was brought forth, when there were no springs abounding with water; [25] before the mountains were settled in place, before the hills, I was brought forth, [26] before he made the earth or its fields or any of the dust of the world. [27] I was there when he set the heavens in place, when he marked out the horizon on the face of the deep, [28] when he established the clouds above and fixed securely the fountains of the deep, [29] when he gave the sea its boundary so the waters would not overstep his command, and when he marked out the foundations of the earth. [30] Then I was beside him, like a master workman. I was filled with delight day after day, rejoicing always in his presence, [31] rejoicing in his whole world and delighting in the children of man. [32] "And now, my sons, listen to me; blessed are those who keep my ways. [33] Listen to my instruction and be wise;

do not ignore it. [34] Blessed is the man who listens to me, watching daily at my doors, waiting at my doorway. [35] For whoever finds me finds life and receives favor from the Lord. [36] But whoever fails to find me harms himself; all who hate me love death."

The *everlasting* Torah existed before the world's creation (John 1:1-4):

[1] In the beginning was the Word, and the Word was with God, and the Word was God. [2] He was with God in the beginning. [3] Through him all things were made; without him nothing was made that has been made. [4] In him was life, and that life was the light of men.

Jesus and the Covenant

In his Gospel, John used the Greek word *Logos*, which relates to the word/reason and is rather impersonal. In the Greek mind, *Logos* (or *logos*) is not preexistent. While writing in Greek, John has brought his Jewish reasoning and Hebrew meaning of the word *logos*: *Memra*, Aramaic for *Maamar* in Hebrew. *Memra* is the creative and directive word of God, used in place of the word "Lord" in Targum (Targum is Aramaic "translation" or "interpretation"; translations to Aramaic were used to paraphrase and make commentary). In the Targum, *Memra* always represents the manifestation of divine power, or God's messenger. It is much weightier than *Logos* and is parallel to the divine Wisdom: His word, the Law. According to this connotation Jesus is the personification of the divine word, His Law (Torah), and Wisdom. Thus, when someone teaches that the Law (Torah) is abrogated, that person contradicts John's teaching since the Lord Jesus could not abolish Himself.

Consequently, avoiding the study of the Torah eliminates aspects of Jesus' influence in the lives of His believers.

See Isa. 2:2-4:

[2] And in the last days the mountain of the Lord's house will be established as chief among the mountains; it will be raised above the hills, and all *Gentiles* [Goyim] will stream to it. [3] And many peoples will come and say, "Come, let us go up to the mountain

of the Lord, to the house of the God of Jacob. He will teach us his ways, so that we may walk in his paths." *The Law* [Torah] will go out from Zion, the word of the Lord from Jerusalem. [4] He will judge between the Gentiles [Goyim] and will settle disputes for many peoples. They will beat their swords into plowshares and their spears into pruning hooks. Nation will not take up sword against nation, nor will they train for war anymore.

Isaiah's prophecy is clear: the Law, the Torah, the Covenant with Israel, and the Messiah Jesus are interconnected.

Faithfulness of God to His Covenant

While examining God's judgment of Israel's faithlessness, the following verses could be cited.

In 1 Kings 19:10-18 Elijah said to God:

[14]...sons of Israel have rejected your covenant, broken down your altars, and put your prophets to death.

To this complaint God replies that there are seven thousand believers remaining in Israel. The God of Israel did not need the compliance of all Israel; the seven thousand were enough to preserve the Covenant.

In Num. 13:25-14:9 only four men—Joshua (Yehoshua) ben Nun, Caleb (Calev) ben Jephunneh, Moses, and Aaron—remained faithful to God. For God, four believers were enough to keep the Covenant valid.

In Ex. 32:1-24 only Moses and Joshua were truly faithful to God, even though the people witnessed the presence of God (Ex. 24:9-11). Nevertheless, 120 believers were enough for the Lord to preserve the Covenant with Israel and Gentile believers as the part of Israel. See Acts 1:15-16:

[15] And in those days Peter stood up among the believers (a crowd of about one hundred and twenty persons was there together), and said [16] Brothers, the Scripture had to be fulfilled which the Holy Spirit spoke long ago through the mouth of David concerning Judas, who served as guide for those who arrested Jesus.

Soon after thousands were added to the first believers (Acts 2:41):

> [41] And those who accepted his message were baptized, and about three thousand were added to their number that day.

Subsequently, thousands more were added, as described in Acts 4:4:

> [4] But many who heard the message believed, and the number of men grew to about five thousand.

Luke states that a multitude of Jews in Jerusalem believed in Jesus, thus they were perceived as competitors by the Temple authorities, and eventually the beginning of the persecution took place in Acts 4:15-21. For the sake of the new believers neither the Law, nor the Covenant were abolished.

Unfaithfulness of all Israel and God's rejection of Israel, as the punishment for unfaithfulness, are supported only by those willing to separate the Lord and Israel.

Undoubtedly, Israel has breached her Covenant obligations, and broken them repeatedly. God judged the Covenant's violations in two quite different ways: God punished Israel the way it was stipulated in the Covenant, and God made *additional* Covenants with Israel.

The creation of additional Covenants was made according to God's mercy, not Israel's merit. Israel received God's grace long before the birth of the modern Church.

Promise of the New Covenant

The idea of the termination of the Covenant with Israel is based only on the penalties for transgressions of the Law. Denying the Lord's grace toward Israel contradicts the Biblical narrative and God's character, and implies that grace is revealed only in New Testament times.

The prophet Jeremiah amplified the Covenant with Israel with the New Covenant (Jer. 31:31-37):

> [31] "The time is coming," declares the Lord, "when I will make a New Covenant with the house of Israel and with the house of Judah. [32] It will not be like the Covenant I made with their fathers

when I took them by the hand to lead them out of Egypt, because they broke my Covenant, though I was their master" declares the Lord. [33] "This is the Covenant I will make with the house of Israel after that time," declares the Lord. "I will put my Law in their minds and write it on their hearts. I will be their God, and they will be my people. [34] And no longer will a man teach his neighbor, and a man his brother, saying, 'Know the Lord,' because they will all know me, from the least of them to the greatest," declares the Lord. "For I will forgive their wickedness and will remember their sins no more." [35] This is what the Lord says, he who appoints the sun to shine by day, who decrees the moon and stars to shine by night, who stirs up the sea so that its waves roar; the Lord Almighty is his name: [36] "Only if these decrees vanish from my sight," declares the Lord, "will the offspring of Israel ever cease to be a nation before me." [37] This is what the Lord says: "Only if the heavens above can be measured and the foundations of the earth below be searched out will I reject all the offspring of Israel because of all they have done," declares the Lord.

Since the Abrahamic, Sinaitic, and Moab Covenants are everlasting, they will never be rescinded. The God of Abraham, Isaac, and Jacob is still the God of Israel, and Israel is still God's people.[22]

Summary of the Covenant with Israel

This analysis of the Covenant with Israel has shown that:

- The Covenant is everlasting
- Blessings are associated with the keeping the Covenant, and punishment is associated with breaking the Covenant
- The Covenant was not given to people for the purpose of salvation
- The Covenant is needed so that Israel may know that it is the Lord who sanctifies Israel
- In response to breaches of the Covenant, God has made additional Covenants with Israel, which demonstrate the character of God.

---

22 Stephen J. Binz, Sacred Heart of Jesus (2006) 23.

Isaiah's Covenant

Another *everlasting* Covenant with Isaiah connects Israel with the Messiah (Isa. 59:20-21):

> [20] "The Redeemer will come to Zion, to those in Jacob who repent of their sins," declares the Lord. [21] "As for me, this is my Covenant with them," says the Lord. "My Spirit, who is on you, and my words that I have put in your mouth will not depart from your mouth, or from the mouths of your offspring, or from the mouths of your offspring's offspring from this time on and *forever*," says the Lord.

This *everlasting* Covenant comes to mind when someone intentionally claims that only "earthly" Covenants were made with Jews.

Mosaic Law

According to rabbinical teaching Mosaic Law includes 613 commandments, which are found from Gen. 17:10 to Deut. 28:68. The Ten Commandments are given separately on Mount Sinai by God Himself. The 613 commandments are categorized into "to do" commandments (247) and "do not" commandments (365), along with the First commandment. Therefore, the view of the Law as based on the works is incorrect; there are more prohibitive commandments than "to do" commandments in the Law.

The number 613 is given in the Talmud (Makkot 23b), but the commandments themselves have not been compiled into a single list. According to rabbinic teaching, 248 is the number of bones in the human body, and 365 is the number of days in a year, and these numbers have mystical meanings.

The listing of commandments was initially made by Maimonides in roughly 1170 A.D., where some of the commandments are his interpretations of the Biblical text. At the same time, the list of commandments was inflated intentionally: some of the commandments were divided in two. Since it was not sufficient to bring the number of commandments to 613, Maimonides then subdivided some commandments into three.

In other cases, he simply repeated one of the commandments twice and added a "commandment" unsupported by interpretation of the text in Deut. 10:20.

There are no curses or blessings in the commandments of the Law, but incentives for compliance with the Law itself, and penalties for intentional non-compliance. The teachings in some denominations about the Law, in most cases, violate at least one of the commandments, and sometimes more. For example, the Epistle of Barnabas, included into the early writings of the Church Fathers writings (dated 130 A.D.), states that Moses broke the stone tablets and the Covenant with Israel was rejected (Epistle of Barnabas, 4.8): "And Moses understood and cast the two tables out of his hands, and their covenant was broken in pieces." In the Epistle the following out of the Ten Commandments were broken: perjury (the ninth commandment), envy (in this case, envy of Israel's blessings, the tenth commandment), the declaration of the Sabbath as invalid (the fourth commandment), and the attachment of God's name to what He did not say (the third commandment). The First commandment was also broken. The basis for such conclusions is in the Bible: Moses receives tablets (Ex. 24:12, 31:18) and breaks them (Ex. 32:19). But *afterward* Moses receives new copies instead of broken ones (Ex. 34:1, 4, 28), with inscriptions made by God once again. In conclusion, God confirmed His Covenant.

The *full* observance of *all* the commandments is impossible in principle and it is not required. For example, it is almost always impossible for a person not to gossip. Subsequently, some commandments present goals set for believers' behavior and community. When observance of the commandments contradicts one another, the advantage is given to the "weightier" (heavier), more important commandment. Saving a human life is *always* weightier than all other commandments, though the commandments to have faith in God are ultimately the weightiest ones.

Among all God's commandments, the Ten regulate relationships with God and with other people (Deut. 5:5-22):

> [5] And he said:
> I. [6] I am the Lord your God, who brought you out of the land of

Egypt, out of the house of slavery.

II. [7] You shall have no other gods before my face.

III. [11] You shall not say the name of the Lord your God as empty.

IV. [12] Keep the Sabbath day.

V. [16] Honor your father and your mother.

VI. [17] You shall not murder.

VII. [18] You shall not commit adultery.

VIII.[19] You shall not steal.

IX. [20] You shall not bear false witness against your neighbor.

X. [21] You shall not covet anything that belongs to your neighbor.

[22] These words said the Lord.

It is easy to determine a person's spiritual condition based on the Ten commandments, as it is impossible to conceal the breaking of these commandments for an extended period of time, and it is very difficult to pretend to observe the commandments. Lack of faith will always be obvious in the sight of the Lord.

The verse Deut. 5:22, which marks the *end* of the Ten Commandments, uses the Hebrew word *davar*. Davar represents not only a word, but also a statement. In Ex. 20:1 the word *davarim* (plural "the words"), marks the *beginning,* and in Deut. 5:22 the *end* of the Ten Commandments. Accordingly, the verses from Deut. 5:6-21 were written on the stone tablets by God.

Assigning the commandments to different categories, and in a particular order, is purely arbitrary. It is often difficult to classify commandments into a single group; for example, where commandments are arbitrarily divided into ceremonial, legal, and moral, where does the commandment "not to spare Ammonites" belong? Besides, it is impossible to carry out this commandment due to the absence of Ammonites in the past three thousand years. In the past, obviously, the commandment was observed diligently.

Some of the commandments of the Law cannot be kept because of the absence of the Temple, a few commandments almost duplicate each other, some nations and countries no longer exist, and modern society has changed drastically from agrarian to information technology society. Some commandments can be kept only in the land of Israel, and the majority of commandments today may be studied only as a part of history.

The allusion to the "fearsome and unbreachable" wall of the Law in some teachings, which divides Jews and Gentiles, is not based on reality, but more importantly, is not Biblical. For example, today the Jewish population in America is steadily increasing due to intermarriages between Jews and Gentiles, sixty percent of whom accept Judaism as well as the growth of African-American synagogues.

Much that was regulated by the Law in ancient history is regulated much more cheaply, quickly, and efficiently in modern society. For example, the state of Israel is not an absolute monarchy, but rather a democratic republic with a strong middle class.

In addition, some of the commandments which should be observed today might present a challenge. As an illustration, the believers are commanded to obey one of the commandments of the Law: to *study* diligently the word of God (Deut. 6:6-7):

> [6] And these words that I give you today are to be on your heart. [7] and teach them your children. And talk about them when you sit at home and when you walk along the road, when you lie down and when you get up.

Of course, the Law is given to Israel, and therefore it regulates the life and worship of Israel. However, there is a significant difference between the Covenant and the Law. One may conclude:

- The Law is given to Israel, and only Israel determines its meaning.
- There is one, the First commandment, being observed by God (Ex. 20:2)
- Some commandments set up objectives for behavior
- Some commandments are everlasting or provisional
- The commandments of the Law prohibit sinful behavior
- Some of the Law's commandments were broken even before the Law was given to Israel
- Some commandments are meant only for Israel, and others given to all people

- Some commandments cannot be abrogated, and they are observed today.

Based on the above, it becomes clear that the Covenant with Israel and the Law are not identical concepts.

This reasoning helps to define the basis of the identification of the Law and the Covenant. Some people argue that the history of Israel began on Mount Sinai. As shown above, this is erroneous. Based on the Biblical narrative, Jewish history began much earlier, in the time of the patriarchs. God made many Covenants with Israel, and all of them are *everlasting*. The proponents of the exclusion of Israel are willing to disregard the existence of separate Covenants, stating that all of them belong to one large Covenant.

There is also a teaching that the Covenant with Israel is synonymous with the Law, where this refers to Moses and the Law of Moses.[23] Thus, both the Law and the Covenant with Israel may be declared annulled. This serves the Church as justification to be without Jews and to avoid the Jewish roots of Christian faith. The Bible is presented as the book for the Church. In Reform terminology, the end result will be a "commonwealth of Israel" without Israel, misinterpreting Eph. 2:12:

> [12] At that time you [Gentiles] were without Christ, excluded from the citizenship of Israel, and foreigners to the covenants of promise, without hope and without God in the world.

As the consequence of Replacement Theology, Gentiles would continue to be separated from Israel and from the Jewish Messiah.

To justify the teaching on abrogation of the Law and the Covenant with Israel, Gal. 3:10, 14 are frequently cited:

> [3:10] And all who rely on works of the Law are under a curse...
> [14] so that in Christ Jesus the blessing of Abraham might come to the Gentiles, so that we might receive the promised Spirit through faith.

---

23 Frank Thielman, Paul & the Law: A Contextual Approach (1994) 220; Tim F. LaHaye, Edward E. Hindson, The Popular Bible Prophecy Commentary: Understanding the Meaning of every prophetic passage (2007) 473.

But works of the Law without faith are not what God requires. He desires willful obedience for human good, not a new slavery. Jewish history, like any history, abounds in dependence on outer compliance paired with a reliance on manmade theories.

The essence of the verses is that unbelievers are not able to keep the Law without breaking it, but believers in God can. Consequently, those who want to abolish the Law profess that they do not believe in what is written in the Bible. According to Scripture, Gentile believers receive the blessings of Abraham because they are part of Israel.

Some teachings define the Law as a yoke. The Lord commands that the Law be followed always (Deut. 11:1):

> [1] And love the Lord your God and keep his requirements, his decrees, his laws and his commands *always*.

Deut. 5:29:

> [59] Oh, that their hearts would be inclined to fear me and keep all my commands always, so that it might go well with them and their children *forever*!

Ps. 119:127:

> [127] Because I love your commands more than gold, more than pure gold,

It is critical for a believer to love and keep the Law, because the Law *exonerates* believers and *condemns* unbelievers.

Mosaic Law and Gentiles

The Old Testament states that the Law of Moses is compatible with Gentiles in Isa. 56:1-8:

> [1] Thus says the Lord: "Keep justice, and do righteousness, for soon my salvation will come, and my righteousness be revealed.
> [2] Blessed is the man who does this, and the son of man who holds

it fast, who keeps the Sabbath, not profaning it, and keeps his hand from doing any evil." ³ Let not the Gentile[24] who has joined himself to the Lord say, "The Lord will surely separate me from his people"; and let not the eunuch say, "Behold, I am a dry tree." ⁴ For thus says the Lord: "To the eunuchs who keep my Sabbaths, who choose the things that please me and hold fast my covenant, ⁵ I will give in my house and within my walls a monument and a name better than sons and daughters; I will give them an everlasting name that shall not be cut off. ⁶ "And the Gentiles who join themselves to the Lord, to minister to him, to love the name of the Lord, and to be his servants, everyone who keeps the Sabbath and does not profane it, and holds fast my covenant: ⁷ these I will bring to my holy mountain, and make them joyful in my house of prayer; their burnt offerings and their sacrifices will be accepted on my altar; for my house shall be called a house of prayer for all peoples." ⁸ The Lord God, who gathers the outcasts of Israel, declares, "I will gather yet others to him besides those already gathered."

This points to the New Testament, especially, if we emphasize "my salvation will come." The Hebrew name Yeshua (in Greek, "Jesus") means "God saves." While cleansing His Temple from moneychangers, Jesus said (Matt. 21:13):

> ¹³ It is written, my house will be called a house of prayer, but you are making it a den of thieves!

What was good for Jesus should be good for His Church. Isaiah speaks about revolutionary changes in the understanding of Mosaic Law. For example, the Law prohibits eunuchs to enter the assembly of the Lord (Deut. 23:1). Isaiah predicts that the Messiah will establish the mercy of salvation through faith. It is of utmost importance for all, as was said by Paul in Eph. 2:11-16 (in full agreement with Isa. 56:8).

It would be no exaggeration to say that the prophecy of Isaiah puts Pharisees and Sadducees on a collision course with Jesus. The prophecy is applied in Acts 8:26-40, where an angel of the Lord guides Philip to meet a eunuch. The eunuch, who undoubtedly knew what was written in Isa. 56:1-8 suggested to Philip: "See, here is water! What

---

24 Foreigner in Hebrew.

prevents me from being baptized?" And Philip, with his knowledge of Scripture, answered "you may."

The Law of Moses and the New Covenant

A significant number of Christians believe that the Law of Moses has no validity in New Testament times. They might have heard the statements that Jesus rejected Mosaic Law and gave two new commandments instead: to love God and to love your neighbor. On the contrary, the Law is deeply intertwined with the New Covenant. Moreover, the Law is prevalent in the teaching of Jesus and the Apostles.

Jesus and the Law

Matt. 12:1-14 is often cited to justify abolishing Mosaic Law.

First, see Matt. 12:1-8:

> 12:1 At that time Jesus went through the grain fields on the Sabbath. And his disciples were hungry and began to pick some heads of grain and eat them. 2 And when the Pharisees saw this, they said to him, "Look, your disciples are doing what is not lawful on the Sabbath." 3 He said to them, "Haven't you read what David did when he and his companions were hungry? 4 He entered the house of God, and he and his companions ate the consecrated bread: which was not lawful for them to do, but only for the priests. 5 Or haven't you read in the Law that on the Sabbath the priests in the Temple desecrate the day and yet are innocent? 6 I tell you something greater than the temple is here. 7 If you had known what these words mean, 'I desire mercy, not sacrifice,' you would not have condemned the innocent. 8 For the Son of Man is Lord of the Sabbath."

This text is structured in the following order: the description, the first evidence, the second evidence, the first conclusion, the second conclusion.

The description of the event (Matt. 12:1-2):

It was summertime, when the grain is about to ripen. It might be the afternoon on a Sabbath day. The disciples have already walked almost all the distance to the village, violating the Sabbath travel limit, though this was done by Jesus' consent. Tearing off ears of grain and cleaning them from their awns is forbidden on Sabbath, but Jesus has allowed that too. An exception to the rules could only be made if the lives of the disciples were in danger (Ex. 20:10). But they might easily endure hunger until sunset, about nine hours later. The Pharisees were definitely correct regarding Jesus' disciples breaking the Law.

Did these Pharisees accompany Jesus and disciples? No, they could not violate the ban on crossing distances of more than 1,200 yards on Saturdays and thus they came from this local settlement.

The first evidence (Matt. 12:3-4):
The theological dispute commences quickly over the observance of the Sabbath. The story of the bread from the Temple was told in 1 Sam. 21:1-6, and the broken commandment of the Law is found in Lev. 24:5-9. The comparison of both cases is done in accordance with the rule *gezera shava*. Both cases have a similarity in which they are compared: grain or bread and hunger. The High Priest in Lev. 24:5-9 was also familiar with the Law but came to a completely different decision than the Pharisees. And Jesus based his evidence on the decision of the High Priest, which had been known already for a thousand years.

The second evidence (Matt. 12:5):
The priests in the Temple indeed worked on Saturdays, according to the commandment to burn incense twice a day (Ex. 30:7-8). This commandment takes precedence over observance of the Sabbath, because in Judaism, if the observance of the commandments contradicts each other, the more important, "weightier" commandment is kept. Jesus defines this logic: if the Temple is more important than the Sabbath, then mercy is more important than the Temple. It is based on the following reasoning: God's mercy precedes the Temple's construction.

The first conclusion (Matt. 12:6-7):
The quotation itself is from Hos. 6:6, but is amplified by the accusing context of Hos. 6:4-6.

> [4] "What can I do with you, Ephraim? What can I do with you, Judah? Your love is like the morning mist, like the early dew that disappears. [5] Therefore I cut you in pieces with my prophets, I

killed you with the words of my mouth; my judgments flashed like lightning upon you. ⁶ For I desire mercy, not sacrifice, and knowledge of God rather than burnt offerings.

To judge a person is also forbidden on Sabbath. Condemning an innocent person is a much heavier sin. Thus, Jesus declared that those Pharisees did sin and transgressed the Law. Only God alone could be higher than the Temple.

The second conclusion (Matt. 12:8):
This statement is essential for understanding what has happened. Jesus confirms that He has the right to allow His disciples to infringe the Sabbath. God declared "I want mercy," exercising His right as the creator. Jesus is the Lord of Sabbath Himself.

We turn now to Matt. 12:9-14:

> ⁹ And going on from that place, he went into their synagogue, ¹⁰ and a man with a shriveled hand was there. And looking for a reason to accuse Jesus, they asked him, saying "Is it lawful to heal on the Sabbath?" ¹¹ And he said to them, "If any of you has a sheep and it falls into a pit on the Sabbath, will you not take hold of it and lift it out? ¹² How much more valuable is a man than a sheep! Therefore it is lawful to do good on the Sabbath." ¹³ Then he said to the man, "Stretch out your hand." And he stretched it out and it was completely restored, just as sound as the other. ¹⁴ And the Pharisees went out and plotted how they might kill Jesus.

The text is structured in the following order: the description, the third evidence, the fourth evidence, and the final conclusion.

The description (Matt. 12:9-10):
Jesus came to a synagogue full of people, where there was a man with a shriveled arm. The Pharisees, having lost the previous dispute, fully understood the consequences of Jesus' teaching. They provoked a new dispute on the Law and Sabbath. They obviously could not foresee that the events would move from words to action. Since the man with the shriveled arm in this gathering was not on the brink of death, they were expecting a negative answer, as it was prohibited to heal on Sabbath.

The third evidence (Matt. 12:11-12).
Jesus quotes the commandment of the Law from Ex. 23:5 namely, if you see your enemy's donkey fallen, help it. In this case the rule *kal vachomer* is applied. If someone is allowed to help a suffering animal on Sabbath, how much more he needs to help people any day of a week.

The fourth evidence (Matt. 12:13):
This is particularly important because it's based on a miracle, not a quotation from the Bible. The hand has likely been withered by nerve or joint damage, followed by muscular atrophy. First, the person stretched out his hand, either by himself or by supporting it with another hand, and then, in front of everybody, the hand suddenly becomes healthy and muscles grow on it. Modern medicine is unable to recreate this healing process. The Bible gives examples of the miracles performed either by God Himself or through a prophet.

The final conclusion (Matt. 12:14).
The Pharisees witnessed the unique miracle, realized that they were dealing with the prophet, and planned to kill him. This alone is the proof of their own unbelief in God.

Jesus taught about the Mosaic Law in His Sermon on the Mount (Matt. 5:19):

> ¹⁹ And anyone who *loosen* one of the least of these commandments and teaches others to do the same will be called least in the kingdom of heaven, and whoever practices and teaches these commands will be called great in the kingdom of heaven.

Matt. 7:12:

> ¹² Therefore, whatever you want others to do for you, do also the same for them, for this is the Law and the Prophets.

In Matt. 26:59-60, during the trial of Jesus, the accusers did not put forward events in Matt. 12:1-14 and could not even find any false testimony to condemn Jesus. However, the call to abrogate the Law was the violation of the commandment and punished by the death penalty. It's hard to comprehend, but what His enemies did not dare to bring up as accusation became the so-called teaching on annulment of the Law by Jesus and accepted by various Churches.

After His resurrection from the dead, Jesus spent forty days teaching the first Christians (Acts 1, 1 Cor. 15:2-7). The First Church met in the Temple (Acts 2:46), and continued to observe the commandments of the Mosaic Law (Acts 1:12):

> [12] Then they returned to Jerusalem from the hill called the Mount of Olives, a Sabbath day's walk from the city.

The commandment limits Saturday's walk distance. Most of the commandments are optional for Gentile believers, but they were strictly mandatory for the Jews in the first century. Hence, the Law does not forbid Gentiles to believe in God *together* with Israel, but no one has ever given Gentiles any authority to practice their faith being without of Israel.

Apostles and the Law

Acts 10:9-17:

> [10:9] And the following day as they were on their journey and approaching the city, Peter went up on the roof about the sixth hour to pray. [10] And it come to pass that he became hungry and wanted something to eat, and while the meal was being prepared, he fell into a trance. [11] And he saw heaven opened and something like a large sheet being let down to earth by its four corners. [12] It contained all kinds of four-footed animals, as well as reptiles of the earth and birds of the air. [13] And it come to pass that a voice told him, "Get up, Peter. Kill and eat." [14] And Peter replied "Surely not, Lord! I have never eaten anything impure or unclean." [15] And the voice spoke to him a second time, "Do not call anything impure that God has made clean." [16] And it come to pass three times, and immediately the sheet was taken back to heaven. [17] While Peter was wondering about the meaning of the vision, the men sent by Cornelius found out where Simon's house was and stopped at the gate.

Some commentaries interpret God's words in verse 13 as permission for Peter to eat unclean animals. If one accepts this interpretation, God overturns all of the Old Testament dietary laws according to verse 15. Following this interpretation God annulled His own Law, and this decision consequently broke His Covenant with Israel.

It should be noted that the commandments about kosher food were *never expected* to be kept by Gentiles.

In Jewish traditions of the first century A.D., many practices of Gentiles were considered "common" or unclean. Peter was not expected to enter the house of Cornelius (Acts 10:28):

> [28] And he said to them: "You are well aware that it is not acceptable for a Jew to associate with a Gentile or visit him..."

The vision from the Lord broke down the dividing wall that man-made rabbinical traditions had built. This barrier severely hindered the spread of the Gospel to the Gentiles. God's teaching for Israel being holy and set apart should not present a conflict for Israel to be a light for the Gentiles (Isa. 42:6):

> [6] I, the Lord, have called you in righteousness; I will take hold of your hand. I will keep you and will make you to be a covenant for the people and a light for the Gentiles,

Isa. 49:6:

> [6] I will also make you a light for the Gentiles, that you may bring my salvation to the ends of the earth."

Description of clean and unclean food was given in Lev. 11:1-23 and Deut. 14:3-21. Peter did not interpret the vision as given about non-kosher food, Acts 10:28:

> [28] ...But God has shown me that I should not call man impure or unclean.

Peter, other disciples and the early Church as a whole acted right on the message (Acts 11:11-18):

> [18] And when they heard this, they quieted down and glorified God, saying, "So then, *God has granted to Gentiles repentance into life.*"

The vision was soon to bring Peter to meet Cornelius and his family and friends.

The Apostle John demonstrated his beliefs on the Law (1 John 2:3-4):

> [3] And we know that we have come to know him if we obey his commandments. [4] The man who says, "I know him," but does not keep His commandments is a liar, and the truth is not in him.

1 John 3:4-6:

> [4] Everyone who sins breaks the Law; in fact, sin is without Law. [5] And you know that he appeared so that he might take away our sins. And in him is no sin. [6] No one who lives in him sins. No one who continues to sin has either seen him or known him.

Rev. 22:18-19:

> [18] I warn everyone who hears the words of the prophecy of this book: If anyone adds anything to them, God will add to him the plagues described in this book. [19] And if anyone takes words away from this book of prophecy, God will take away from him his share in the tree of life and in the holy city, which are described in this book.

It is forbidden to include one's own writings into the Bible and the Law, or exclude any part. These Mosaic commandments of the Law are reinforced by God in Deut. 4:2 and 12:32.

Paul and the Law

Being a disciple of Jesus, Paul would not contradict the words of his master in Rom. 3:31:

> [31] Do we then overthrow the law by this faith? By no means! On the contrary, we uphold the law.

Since the Gospel of Matthew was written later, Paul did not refer to Matt. 5:17. He was introduced to the teachings by Apostles in the First Church.

Based on this teaching, if Paul strived to be great, he had to both observe the Law and *teach* others to keep commandments as well. Paul did both according to Biblical evidence.

However, there have been some suggestions about Paul's presumed commercial activities in Biblical commentaries. We read in Acts 18:2-3:

> [18:2] And there he met a Jew named Aquila, a native of Pontus, who had recently come from Italy with his wife Priscilla, because Claudius had ordered all the Jews to leave Rome. Paul went to see them, [3] and because he was of the same trade as they were, he stayed and worked with them, and by trade they were *sukkah*-makers.

The word used here, *skenopoioi*, means "maker of skene." *Skene* is mentioned in the Septuagint, and in Hebrew it is a *sukkah*, plural *sukkot*. In Heb. 9:3 *skene* was translated as "tabernacle," or *mishkan* in Ex. 26:9 in Hebrew. Thus, the two Hebrew words were translated into Greek as *skene*.

On this feast of Sukkot, the Jews built *sukkot*, which represent *mishkan*, temporary collapsible structures. According to tradition, it is necessary to spend at least one hour a day in it eating a small meal. Usually, a few *sukkot* were installed next to the synagogue, and both the making of *sukkot* and their assembly were reserved for Jews with an impeccable religious reputation. As is widely known, both Paul and Aquila were known to be flawless in their keeping the Law of Moses. Paul also took the Nazarene oath, which confirms his special dedication to keeping the Law.

It is interesting that in 2 Cor. 5:1 Paul compares the human body with the *sukkah*, which is a very temporary and flimsy dwelling place:

> [1] And we know that if the earthly shelter, *sukkah*, is destroyed, we have a building from God, an eternal house in heaven, not built by human hands.

In the Letter to the Galatians, Paul builds his logic on the idea that the Covenant with Israel and the Law continue to be in force. Luke, Paul's companion, recorded the following in Acts 24:20:

> [20] Or these who are here should state what crime they *found in me*

when I stood before the Sanhedrin.

Acts 25:8:

> [8] Then Paul made his defense: "I have done *nothing wrong* against the Law of the Jews or against the Temple."

Acts 26:22:

> [22] And I have had God's help to this very day, and so I stand here and testify to small and great alike. I am *saying nothing* beyond what the prophets and Moses said would happen.

He speaks in a synagogue in Acts 13:5, 43:

> [5] And it come to pass when they arrived at Salamis, they proclaimed the word of God in the Jewish synagogues. John was with them as their helper...
> [43] And when the congregation was dismissed, many of the Jews and God-fearing proselytes followed Paul and Barnabas, who talked with them and urged them to continue in the grace of God.

If he were calling for abolishing the Law or abandoning Judaism, he would not have even been allowed to enter the synagogue, and in all likelihood would have been stoned.

The Church in Jerusalem was concerned about the *libel* that Paul proposed to stop keeping the Law, and thus made an effort to demonstrate that Paul continued to be an exemplary Jew (Acts 21:20):

> [20] And when they heard this, they praised God. Then they said to Paul: You see, brother, how many myriads of Jews have believed, and all of them are *zealous for the Law*.

Acts 21:24:

> [24] Take these men, join in their purification rites and pay their expenses, so that they can have their heads shaved. And then everybody will know there is no truth in these reports about you, but that you yourself walk orderly, *keeping the Law*.

Acts 21:26:

> [26] The next day Paul took the men and *purified himself* along with them. Then he went to the Temple to give notice of the date when the days of purification would end, and the *sacrifice* would be made for each of them.

These ideas are anything but new. Rabbi Simeon ben Zemah Duran (1361-1444) in his polemical work against Christianity titled *Keshet U-Magen* stated:

> And it is also written by Luke [Acts 28:17-18] that when one of the Apostles [Paul] was brought to Rome, bound in chains, he called to the Jews who were there and said to them that he had not done anything against the Jews, and that he did not differ at all with their ancestral custom. He also said that the Jews of Jerusalem had not found in him anything deserving of the death penalty. And had he differed with the Torah, he would have been deserving of the death penalty. And similarly, he wrote in one of his books that he believes in everything which is in the Torah.[25]

The book was translated into English in 1975.

Church and the Law

Prior to Paul's second journey, the decisions of the Apostles and elders concerning Gentile Christians were based on the commandments of Mosaic Law (Acts 15:28-29):

> [28] And it seemed good to the Holy Spirit and to us not to burden you with anything beyond the following requirements: [29] that you are to abstain from food sacrificed to idols, from blood, from the meat of strangled animals and from sexual immorality. You will do well to avoid these things.

Acts 18:8 describes the addition of the head of the synagogue as well as many other members of the same synagogue to faith in the Messiah. They did not stop to observe the Law.

---

25 Juan Marcos Bejarano Gutierrez, Forgotten Origins: The Lost Jewish History of Jesus and Early Christianity (2018) 20.

[8] Crispus, the synagogue ruler, and his entire household believed in the Lord; and many of the Corinthians who heard him believed and were baptized.

The extent to which the commandments of the Mosaic Law fill out most books of the New Testament needs to be emphasized.

A good example is found in James 2:2-12:

[2] And if a man comes into your *synagogue* wearing gold ring and sparkling white clothes, and a poor man in shabby clothes also comes in. [3] And you show special attention to the man wearing sparkling white clothes and say, "Here's a good seat for you," and say to the poor man, "You stand there" or "Sit on the floor by my feet," [4] have you not discriminated among yourselves and become judges with evil thoughts? [5] Listen, my beloved brothers: Has not God chosen those who are poor in the eyes of the world to be rich in faith and to inherit the kingdom he promised those who love him? [6] And you have insulted the poor. Is it not the rich who are exploiting you? Are they not the ones who are dragging you into court? [7] Are they not the ones who are slandering the noble name of him to whom you belong? [8] If you really keep the royal Law found in Scripture, "Love your neighbor as yourself," you are doing right. [9] And if you show favoritism, you sin and are convicted by the Law as transgressors. [10] And whoever keeps the whole Law and yet stumbles at just one point is guilty of breaking all of it. [11] And he who said, "Do not commit adultery," and said, "Do not murder." If you do not commit adultery and do commit murder, you have become a lawbreaker. [12] Speak and act as those who are going to be judged by the Law that gives freedom...

The Law of Moses forbids taking the side of the rich (Lev. 19:15). Consequently, believers in this synagogue, as James purposefully calls this Church, transgress the Law of Moses. As a rule, the Jews do not come to a synagogue dressed in an unashamedly opulent manner. The verse on the commandment to love your neighbor as yourself (Lev. 19:18), belongs to the royal Law. It turns as the condemning Law to some people who do not abide in it, and it is the easily kept Law of freedom to others.

In his letters Paul often calls believers for life based on the command-ments of the Law (Rom. 1:26-27):

> [26] Because of this, God gave them over to shameful lusts. Even their women exchanged natural relations for unnatural ones. [27] In the same way the men also abandoned natural relations with women and were inflamed with lust for one another. Men commit-ted indecent acts with other men and received in themselves the due penalty for their error.

These types of sexual relations are forbidden in Lev. 18:22.

See Rom. 2:1:

> [2:1] Therefore you have no excuse, every man who passes judgment on someone else, and at whatever point you judge the other, and you are condemning yourself, because you who pass judgment do the same things.

The commandment is to be impartial (Lev. 19:15).

Paul calls to include Gentiles into Israel based on the Moab Covenant (Rom. 2:14):

> [14] And when Gentiles, who do not have the Law, do by nature things required by the Law, they are the Law for themselves, even though they do not have the Law...

It is the commandment to keep the commandments of the Lord your God (Deut. 28:9).

See Rom. 2:23:

> [23] You who brag about the Law, do you dishonor God by breaking the Law?

The commandment is not to blaspheme (Ex. 22:28).

Paul refers to the commandment given to Abraham (Lev. 12:3) in Rom. 2:26, 4:8-11:

> [2:26] And if one who are not circumcised keeps the Law's require-

ments, will not his uncircumcision be regarded as circumcision?... [4:8] Blessed is the man whose sin the Lord will never count against him." [9] And this blessedness given for the circumcised, or for the uncircumcised? And we have been saying that Abraham's faith was credited to him as righteousness. [10] And under what circumstances was it credited? And while he was circumcised, or uncircumcised? Not while circumcised, but uncircumcised. [11] And he received the sign of circumcision, a seal of the righteousness that he had by faith while he was still uncircumcised. So then, he is the father of all who believe without being circumcised, in order that righteousness might be credited to them.

Paul uses it as evidence that believing Gentiles are part of Israel and descendants of Abraham.

Sometimes a reference to the Law can be inconspicuous or implicit (Rom. 6:1):

[1] And what shall we say, then? Shall we go on sinning so that grace may increase?

Failure to obey this commandment leads to a new violation of the Law, which is obviously intentional. Understanding the above as a sign of unbelief in God prepares the reader to proper interpretation of the fifth and sixth chapters of the letter to the Romans.

See Rom. 7:1-3:

[7:1] Do you not know, brothers, and I am speaking to men who know the Law, that the Law has authority over a man only as long as he lives? [2] And by Law a married woman is bound to her husband as long as he is alive, and if her husband dies, she is released from the Law of marriage. [3] And if she marries another man while her husband is still alive, she is called an adulteress. And if her husband dies, she is free by the Law and is not an adulteress, though she is joined to another man.

Paul refers to Ex. 20:14 and Lev. 18:20 as the sin of adultery. The basis of Paul's teaching is the knowledge that the Law was not canceled, but directs the lives of *Gentile* believers as well. On that basis Paul uses *gezera shava* to connect Rom. 7:1-3 and Rom. 7:4-6. The common word "dead" connects both parts of the rule and Paul continues to use it through the rest of the seventh chapter.

As a result, any attempts to annul or make obsolete the Law of Moses lead to rejection of the holy Law of God (Rom. 7:12):

> [12] So then, the Law is holy, and the commandment is holy, and righteous and good.

The commandment to keep the commandments of your God (Deut. 28:9), is the confirmation that the Law is holy, righteous, and good.

See Rom. 8:35:

> [35] Who shall separate us from the love of Christ? Shall tribulation, or distress, or persecution, or famine, or nakedness, or danger, or sword?

The verse refers to the commandment to fear only the Lord, your God (Deut. 10:20).

Rom. 11:11:

> [11] And I say: Did they stumble so as to fall? Not at all! But because of their transgression, salvation has come to the Gentiles to make them [Jews] envious.

This phrase is based on the commandment to love a stranger, a Gentile (Deut. 10:19). Paul applied *kal vachomer* to this commandment: if Jews should love a stranger, how much more should *a stranger love Jews*. And this is the only way to respond to faith in God.

The following verses quote the Isaiah Covenant; Paul confirms that the Covenant with Israel inextricably linked with the Law of Moses and the New Testament (Rom. 11:26-27):

> [26] And so all Israel will be saved, as it is written: "The deliverer will come from Zion; he will turn godlessness away from Jacob. [27] And this is *my covenant* with them when I take away their sins."

Paul refers to Isa. 27:9:

> [9] By this, then, will Jacob's guilt be atoned for, and this will be the full fruitage of the removal of his sin.

See also Isa. 59:20-21:

> [20] "The Redeemer will come to Zion, to those in Jacob who repent of their sins," declares the Lord. [21] "As for me, this is my covenant with them," says the Lord. "My Spirit, who is on you, and my words that I have put in your mouth will not depart from your mouth, or from the mouths of your children, or from the mouths of their descendants from this time on and forever," says the Lord.

Paul brings together the Messianic verse from Isa. 59 and the verse on atonement from Isa. 27, linking this atonement to the New Covenant in Jer. 31:33-34. Paul believes that God is referring specifically to *all* of Israel.

According to Paul it is very easy to observe the Law (Rom. 13:8-9):

> [8] Let no debt remain outstanding, except the continuing debt to love one another, and he who loves the other has fulfilled the Law. [9] The commandments, "Do not commit adultery," "Do not murder," "Do not steal," "Do not covet," and whatever other commandment there may be, are summed up in this one rule: "Love your neighbor as yourself."

The sixth through tenth commandments are found in Ex. 20:13-17 and Deut. 5:17-21. The commandments not to enact revenge, not to have anger against your people, and the commandment to love your neighbor as yourself come from Lev. 19:18.

Rom. 14:13:

> [13] And let us stop passing judgment on one another. But rather determine not to put any stumbling block in a brother's way or make him fall.

This is the commandment not to hate your brother, Lev. 19:17.

See Rom. 15:15-16:

> [15] And I have written you, brothers, quite boldly on some points, as
> if to remind you of them again, because of the grace God gave me
> [16] to be a minister of Christ Jesus to the Gentiles with the priestly
> duty of proclaiming the gospel of God, so that the Gentiles might
> become an offering acceptable to God, sanctified by the Holy
> Spirit.

Logically this is a guilt offering for the sin committed without the
knowledge of the Law (Lev. 5:17-19). The *Gentiles also offered sacrifices, good will offerings*. That was *never forbidden to them*. Surprisingly, a Gentile, even an idol-worshiper, could offer a sacrifice at the
Temple, which was mentioned in the Talmud (Menachot 73b).

The words of Philo, Jesus' contemporary, may bear better witness. In
his work "On the Embassy to Gaius, 157," Philo stated that Roman
emperor Augustus established everyday sacrifice at the Temple, paid
by the emperor as the tribute to the Jewish God.

Whatsoever the reason for sacrifice, God did not reject it.

See Rom. 16:17:

> [17] And I urge you, brothers, to watch out for those who cause divi-
> sions and put obstacles in your way that are contrary to the teach-
> ing you have learned. Keep away from them.

This is correlated to the commandment not to make your brother stumble (Lev. 19:14).

See 1 Cor. 6:15:

> [15] Do you not know that your bodies are members of Christ? Shall
> I then take the members of Christ and make them members of a
> harlot? May it never be!

This is correlated to the forbidding of prostitution in Israel (Deut.
23:17).

See 1 Cor. 7:2:

> [2] And since there is so much immorality, each man should have his own wife, and each woman her own husband.

The commandment to get married, Deut. 22:13.

See 1 Cor. 7:17-19:

> [17] Nevertheless, each one should walk as the Lord assigned to him and as God has called him. And thus I direct in all the churches. [18] Was a man circumcised when he was called? He should not become uncircumcised. Was a man uncircumcised when he was called? He should not be circumcised. [19] Circumcision is nothing and uncircumcision is nothing, but the keeping of the commandments of God.

These verses have a direct connection with the Moab Covenant and confirm the Covenant with Israel and the Law of Moses for the Church.

As we can see, the quantity of quotes from the Law in the New Testament is almost endless. See also 1 Cor. 9:8-9:

> [8] Do I say this merely from a human point of view? And doesn't the Law say the same thing? [9] For it is written in the Law of Moses: "Do not muzzle an ox while it is treading out the grain." Is it about oxen that God is concerned?

This refers to the commandment not to close the mouth of working cattle (Deut. 25:4). In the Law of Moses it applies only to animals, but Paul uses *kal vachomer* and changes the application of the commandment to the preachers of the Gospel, who received no other payment.

See 1 Cor. 10:21:

> [21] You cannot drink the cup of the Lord and the cup of demons, you cannot have a part in the Lord's table and the table of demons.

The *gezera shava* rule is applied to the text of the commandment not to drink the wine offered to an idol (Deut. 32:38).

See 1 Cor. 11:4:

> [4] Every man who prays or prophesies with his head covered dishonors his head.

Where did this come from? The commandment of the Law says that the priest must wear a sacred garment in the Temple (Ex. 28:2). Paul does not want believers in Jesus, especially Gentiles, to be confused with priests in the Temple. This would be a violation of the Law. Wearing a *kippah* (a skullcap) became a common practice for men only in the Middle Ages, long after the destruction of the Temple.

The following standalone verse is particularly important to understand the way that Paul reasoned (1 Cor. 14:21):

> [21] In the Law it is written: "Through men of other tongues and through another lips I will speak to this people, and even then they will not listen to me, says the Lord.

This refers to Isa. 28:11-12:

> [11] Very well then, with stammering lips and another tongue God will speak to this people, [12] to whom he said, "This is the resting place, let the weary rest"; and "Here is repose but they would not listen.

Paul uses *gezera shava*, and his quotation differs slightly from Isaiah's text. The verse is not a commandment of Mosaic Law, obviously, as Isaiah lived more than five centuries after Moses. In the context of the Jewish division of the Bible (Old Testament) into three parts—the Law, the Prophets, and the Writings—Paul refers to the *entire Old Testament as the Law of Moses*. Therefore, when somebody attempts to abolish the Law, this means the invalidation of the *entire* Old Testament which would result in the loss of the New Testament.

The following verses cause many problems for commentators (1 Cor. 14:34-35):

> [34] Let your women be silent in the churches. They are not allowed to speak, but must be in submission, and as the Law says. [35] And if they want to inquire about something, they should ask their own

husbands at home; for it is disgraceful for a woman to speak in the church. [36] Did the word of God went forth from you? Or it has reached only you? [37] If anybody thinks he is a prophet or spiritually gifted, let him acknowledge that what I am writing to you are the Lord's commandments.

Paul's admonition to the Corinthians pertains to maintaining order in worship. It fits within his overall message in 1 Cor. 11-14 regarding order in *ecclesia*. From the architecture of the old synagogues, it is known that men and women were seated separately, with women on a balcony or at the back of the building. Traditionally women visited a synagogue a few times a year, so the section for women in the synagogue was small; they were asked to refrain from talking in full voice to their husbands who sit far from them during the service.

But that advice should not be taken as absolute or out of context. Women did function as spiritual and civic leaders as called by God. To name a few: Deborah (Dvorah) in Judg. 4:4, Miriam (Ex. 15:20), and Hildah (2 Chron. 34:22-28). We find that Paul's own record with women in ministry was clear: Priscilla was one of the leaders of the Church, and Phoebe was a deacon as well as the patron from Cenchreae who delivered Paul's letter to the Romans.

A frequently cited verse is sometimes interpreted as a ban on marriages or any relations with unbelievers (2 Cor. 6:14):

> [14] Do not be unequally yoked with unbelievers. For what do righteousness and what without the Law have in common? Or what fellowship can light have with darkness?

However, the commandment not to follow the customs of idolaters (Lev. 20:23) immediately explains the meaning of Paul's advice. It should be read in the context of 2 Cor. 6:16-18:

> [16] What agreement is there between the Temple of God and idols? And we are the Temple of the living God. As God has said: "I will live with them and walk among them, and I will be their God, and they will be my people." [17] "Therefore come out from them and be separate, says the Lord. And do not touch unclean thing, and I will receive you." [18] "I will be a Father to you, and you will be my sons

and daughters, says the Lord Almighty."

Advice is given to Gentiles who are not yet strong in their faith; this advice is based on Lev. 26:11-12:

> [11] I will put my tabernacle among you, and I will not abhor you. [12] I will walk among you and be your God, and you will be my people.

And is also based on Ezek. 37:27:

> [27] And my tabernacle will be with them; I will be their God, and they will be my people.

While both of these quotations refer to Jews (Lev. 26:13), Paul applies *gezera shava*, thus including the Gentiles who believe in Jesus into Israel.

See also 2 Cor. 11:4:

> [4] And if someone comes to you and preaches another Jesus other than we preached, or if you receive a different spirit from the one you received, or a different gospel from the one you accepted, you put up with it readily enough.

The commandment not to turn to idolatry, Lev. 19:4, equates to belief that preaching the other, non-Biblical Jesus, or different Holy Spirit, or a different Gospel is the form of idolatry.

See 2 Cor. 12:20:

> [20] And I am afraid that when I come I may not find you as I want you to be, and you may not find me as you want me to be. There should not be quarreling, jealousy, anger, factions, slander, gossip, arrogance, disorder.

We find the commandment "do not to bear a grudge against one of your people" (Lev. 19:18).

See 2 Cor. 13:1:

> [1] This will be my third visit to you. "Every matter must be established by the mouth of two or three witnesses."

There should be more than one witness in a court (Deut. 17:6), but the primary reference was made in Mosaic Law (Deut. 19:15),

See Gal. 5:3:

> [3] I testify again to every man, who receives circumcision that he is under obligation to keep the whole Law.

The commandment for circumcision (Lev. 12:3) is observed during the conversion to Judaism.

See Gal. 5:19-21:

> [19] And the acts of flesh are obvious: sexual immorality, impurity, sensuality, [20] idolatry and witchcraft, hatred, discord, jealousy, fits of rage, selfish ambition, dissensions, divisions, [21] envy, drunkenness, orgies, and the like.

Apostle Paul made a large list of commandments of the Law which were mandatory for Gentiles in Galatian Church. In the Epistle Paul defines morals of believers by Mosaic Law.

See also Eph. 4:28-32:

> [28] He who has been stealing must steal no longer, and must work, doing something useful with his own hands, that he may have something to share with those in need. [29] Do not let any unwholesome word come out of your mouth, but only what is helpful for edification according to the need, that it may benefit those who listen. [30] And do not grieve the Holy Spirit of God, with whom you were sealed for the day of redemption. [31] Get rid of all bitterness, and rage, and anger, and brawling, and slander, and all malice. [32] And be kind, compassionate to one another, forgiving each other, and in Christ God forgave you.

Paul wrote that commandments of the Law are the basis for building good Christian character.

See Eph. 5:5-11:

> [5] And this you know with certainty, that no immoral, or impure, or greedy person, such a man is an idolater, has any inheritance

in the kingdom of Christ and God. [6] Let no one deceive you with empty words, and because of such things God's wrath comes on the sons of disobedience. [7] And do not be partners with them. [8] And you were once darkness, and now you are light in the Lord, walk as children of light. [9] And the fruit of the light consists in all goodness, and righteousness, and truth. [10] and find out what pleases the Lord. [11] And have nothing to do with the fruitless deeds of darkness, and rather expose them.

The commandment to destroy idolatry is based on Deut. 12:2-3.

See Eph. 6:1-4:

> [6:1] Children, obey your parents in the Lord, and this is right. [2] *"Honor your father and mother"*—which is the first commandment with a promise, [3] *"that it may go well with you and that you may enjoy long life on the earth."* [4] And fathers, do not exasperate your children, instead, bring them up in the training and instruction of the Lord.

The very first Biblical commandment is to have children (Gen. 1:28). We may find the first commandment with the promise in Ex. 16:29. Israelites would receive the double portion of manna on Friday, if they stay where they were and avoided breaking Sabbath.

The commandment to honor one's father and mother is found only in Ex. 20:12 and Lev. 19:3.

In ancient times, the elderly depended on their male offspring, who would keep their part of the commandment. The death penalty was commanded for the violation of the fifth commandment (Ex. 21:15, 17).

See Phil. 3:9:

> [9] and be found in him, not having a righteousness of my own that comes from the Law, but that which is through faith in Christ, the righteousness from God, by faith.

Mechanical compliance with the Law results in a deliberate violation of the Law of Moses. Observance of the commandment to love the

Lord your God (Deut. 6:5) is the true compliance.

See Col. 3:8:

> [8] And now you put all aside: anger, rage, malice, slander, filthy language from your mouth.

This is correlated with the commandment to not hate your brother (Lev. 19:17).

See Col. 4:1:

> [1] Masters, provide your servants with what is right and fair, and knowing that you have a Master in heaven.

Ex. 21:2-6 calls for being just with servants in accordance with the Law.

See 1 Thess. 4:3-5:

> [3] And it is God's will, your sanctification, that you should avoid sexual immorality; [4] that each of you should learn to control his vessel in holiness and honor, [5] not in passionate lust, and not like the Gentiles, who do not know God.

The commandment regarding any kind of sexual sin is based on Lev. 18:6-28.

See 2 Thess. 3:5:

> [5] And may the Lord direct your hearts into God's love and Christ's perseverance.

The verse directs believers to love the Lord your God as in Deut. 6:5.

The Apostle makes reference to the false teachers of the Law in 1 Tim. 1:7:

> [7] desiring to be teachers of the Law, without understanding either what they are saying or the things about which they make confident assertions.

The Law is good for believers, and brings to judgment those who live in sin (1 Tim. 1:8-10):

> [8] And we know that the Law is good if one uses it properly. [9] We also know that Law is made not for the righteous, but for who are without the Law, and rebels, the ungodly and sinful, the unholy and profane; for those who kill their fathers and mothers, for murderers, [10] for adulterers, perverts, for enslavers and liars and perjurers, and for whatever else is contrary to the sound teaching.

According to the Talmud, the word "enslavers" in verse 10 refers also to kidnapping a person for enslavement (Ex. 20:13). This is one of the examples where Maimonides "padded" the commandment to ensure that he ended up with the number 613.

1 Tim. 1:20:

> [20] Among them are Hymenaeus and Alexander, whom I have handed over to Satan to be taught not to blaspheme.

The verse refers to the commandment to not blaspheme God (Ex. 22:28).

See 1 Tim. 2:9-15:

> [9] And women to dress respectably, with decency and propriety, not with braided hair or gold or pearls or expensive clothes, [10] but with good deeds, appropriate for women who profess to fear God. [11] A woman should learn in quietness, full submission. [12] And I do not permit a woman to teach or to have authority over a man; but she must be silent. [13] And Adam was formed first, then Eve. [14] And Adam was not the one deceived; and it was the woman who was deceived and became a transgressor. [15] And woman will be saved through childbearing, if she continues in faith, and love, and holiness, and sound mind.

Paul expands the reasoning in 1 Cor. 14:34-35. Paul does not refer to the Law, because it has nothing to do with overseers. In his message Paul adds a new subject in v. 15. The Law indeed has the commandment to redeem the firstborn boy (Num. 18:15), but the ransom for girls is not stipulated. Gender inequality was a part of life in ancient society.

See 1 Tim. 3:2-5:

> 2 And the overseer must be above reproach, the husband of one wife, temperate, prudent, respectable, hospitable, able to teach, 3 not given to drunkenness, gentle, not quarrelsome, not a lover of money. 4 He must manage his own household well and see that his children obey him with proper respect. 5 If anyone does not know how to manage his own family, how can he take care of God's church?

Paul reasons on the basis of the commandments in Ex. 21:10 to care for your wife (Deut. 15:11), to help the poor (Ex. 22:22), and not to afflict widows or orphans.

See 1 Tim. 6:10:

> 10 And the love of money is a root of all kinds of evil. Some people by longing for it have wandered from the faith and pierced themselves with many griefs.

See also James 5:4:

> 4 Look! The wages you failed to pay the workmen who mowed your fields are crying out against you. And the cries of the harvesters have reached the ears of the Lord Almighty.

The relevant commandments are to not participate in the robbery of a fellow Jew (Ex. 22:25), and not to withhold payment of an employee (Lev. 19:13).

See James 1:25:

> 25 And the man who looks intently into the perfect Law of liberty, and abides by it, not become a forgetful hearer, but a doer, he will be blessed [by God] in what he does.

The Law of Moses requires keeping the commandments of God (Deut. 28:9).

The complete list of the commandments of the Law referred by the authors of the New Testament is much longer. God's faithfulness to His Laws is tied to the fate of His chosen people forever.

Without the Law

In the New Testament the Greek word *anomos* and its variants are used twenty-nine times. It is comprised of the letter alpha as a negative prefix and the word *nomos*, the Law (the Law of Moses).[26] In the Septuagint the correct translation of the word *anomos* is "without the Law." When it is rendered differently in the New Testament, it is, unfortunately, intentional. Consequently, some traditional teachings contradict the Bible.

Paul used the word *paranomos* to mean being outside of or violating the Law (2 Peter 2:16):

> [16] And he was rebuked for his *violation of the Law* by a donkey, a beast without speech, who spoke with a man's voice and restrained the prophet's madness.

The following is the list of different translations of this original Greek word: NIV, wickedness; NASB, transgression; DRB, folly; KJV, iniquity; NKJV, unrighteousness; NLV, mad course; CEV, evil deed; GNT, sin; HSC, irrationality; NAB, crime; NJB, madness. Not a single Bible version presents the correct translation, because these mistranslations were intended to support Church teachings that originated well beyond the first century. Many popular translations were commissioned by religious authorities and executed by the committees for the utilitarian needs of their denominations.

The verse from Rom. 2:12 can serve as a litmus test to detect many other translations of *anomos* in the New Testament:

> [12] And all who have sinned *without the Law* will also perish *without the Law;* and all who have sinned under the Law will be judged by the Law.

Regardless of the differences in the choice of words, all translations in all languages known to the author *correctly* present Paul's message in this verse.

St. Jerome, the first translator of the Bible, the patron saint of all trans-

---

26 Jean Bottéro, Clarisse Herrenschmidt, Jean Pierre Vernant, Ancestor of the West (2000) 97.

lators, knew how to translate *anomos* in the fourth century.[27] Even the Mormons chose the right meaning in the nineteenth century.[28] The mystery of incorrect translation needs to be solved within the New Testament.[29] In some cases the proper translation was used to avoid "censorship."[30] Some surprising "translation" is found in the Septuagint, the Old Testament in Greek. In the process of the Septuagint's new translation into English, inaccurate translations from the New Testament were transferred to the Old Testament.

Meanwhile, the word *anomos* and words with the same root are found in 273 verses in Septuagint. All of these emphasize the state of sin and violation of the Law. Multiple words and expressions which denote different "shades" of violation of the Law are translated with the single word "sin."[31] Thus, sixteen different Hebrew words were translated as *anomia.*[32]

An example can be found in 1 Peter 2:22:

"He committed no sin, and no deceit was found in his mouth."

The verse is quoted from Isa. 53:9 (LXX), the prophecy of the suffering Messiah (Isa. 53:1-12). Peter replaces the word *anomos* in the Septuagint with the word *amartia*, sin.[33] Given the direct connection between the violation of the Law and the definition of sin, this interpretation is well justified. For example, in Ezek. 18:21 (LXX), the word "sin" is represented by *anomenata*, violation of the Law.

Two rebels were crucified along with Jesus. They opposed Rome and committed murder, and thereby broke the Law (Mark 15:28):

[28] And the scripture was fulfilled which says, "He was counted with ones who are *without the Law*."

---

27 Jerome, Homilies, Volume 2 (60-96) (1966) 51.

28 James Edward Talmage, The articles of faith (1901) 74.

29 John Kevin Coyle, Manichaeism and its legacy (2009) 102.

30 Daniel J. Harrington, The Gospel of Matthew (1991) 108.

31 James B. DeYoung, Homosexuality: contemporary claims examined in light of the Bible (2000) 65-68.

32 Kathy Ehrensperger, J. Brian Tucker, Reading Paul in Context: Explorations in Identity Formation (2010) 122.

33 Donald P. Senior, Daniel J. Harrington, 1 Peter, Jude and 2 Peter (2008.) 75.

This quotation is taken from Isa. 53:12 (LXX), where the Hebrew word *poshaim* for "transgressor or rebel or brigand," was translated as "without the Law." The injustice of the false accusation, and the disbelief in God of Jesus' accusers are described in Mark 14:55-65. God, who gave the Law, could not be counted among those who were without the Law.

Practically every intentionally incorrect translation was intended to exclude the Jewish background and roots of the Bible (Acts 2:23):

> [23] This man was handed over to you by God's predetermined plan and foreknowledge; and you, by the hands of *men without the Law*, put him to death by nailing him to the cross.

People without the Law are Romans,[34] who according to Judaism are idolaters. The inclusion of Gentiles into the crucifixion scene holds them accountable as well, where traditionally Jews were considered the only ones responsible.

Paul places life without the Law on the list of deeds that are incompatible with faith (1 Tim. 1:8-10):

> [8] And we know that the Law is good if one uses it as the Law. [9] We also know that Law is made not for the righteous but for men *without the Law* and rebels, the ungodly and sinful, the unholy and irreligious; for those who kill their fathers or mothers, for murderers, [10] for adulterers and homosexuals, for enslavers and liars and perjurers—and for whatever else is contrary to the sound doctrine.

The contrast between the righteous people who believe in Jesus and the unbelievers who live without the Law is obvious: the Law does not obstruct the lives of believers, but it condemns unbelievers. One of the examples is where Paul circumcised Timothy according with the commandment of the Mosaic Law.

This problem becomes even more evident in 2 Thess. 2:8-9:

> [8] And then the one *without the Law* will be revealed, whom the Lord Jesus will overthrow with the breath of his mouth and destroy

---

34 James D. G. Dunn, The new perspective on Paul (2007) 147.

by the splendor of his coming. [9] He will come in accordance with the work of Satan displayed in all kinds of with all power and signs and false wonders...

The eighth verse serves as a warning to the Church at all times.[35] The Antichrist, who is without the Law, acts accordingly to create a Church completely free from the Law.[36] The rejection of Law quickly became accepted since the fourth century A.D.[37]

The sterner warning is found in the following verse (Matt. 7:23):

[23] Then I will tell them, "I never knew you. Away from me, you do what *without the Law*!"

Thus, according to the words of Jesus, the Law (Mosaic Law) belongs to lives of believers. One short verse sums up all of the teaching up in 1 John 3:4:

[4] Everyone who sins does it *without the Law*; in fact, and sin is what *without [or contrary to] the Law*.

The following verses support the subject as well (Matt. 13:41):

[41] The Son of Man will send out his angels, and they will gather out of his kingdom all that causes sin and all who do *without the Law*.

Matt. 23:28:

[28] And in the same way, on the outside you appear to people as righteous and on the inside you are full of hypocrisy and *without the Law*.

See Matt. 24:12:

[12] Because of the increase of what is *without the Law*, the love of most will grow cold...

35 Fẹmi Adeyẹmi, The new covenant Torah in Jeremiah and the law of Christ in Paul (2006) 96; Jürgen Becker, Paul: Apostle to the Gentiles (1993) 85.

36 David C. Sim, The Gospel of Matthew and Christian Judaism (1998) 206.

37 John F. O'Grady, The Roman Catholic church: its origins and nature (1997) 71.

Luke 22:37:

> [37] And I tell you, that this which is written: And he was numbered with those who are *without the Law* and that which refers to me has its fulfillment.

Rom. 4:7:

> [7] Blessed are they who's life *without the Law* forgiven, whose sins are covered.

See Rom. 6:19:

> [19] I put this in human terms because of the weakness of your flesh. And just as you used to offer the parts of your body in slavery to impurity and *without the Law* into life *without the Law*, so now offer them in slavery to righteousness leading into holiness.

2 Cor. 6:14:

> [14] Do not be unequally yoked together with unbelievers. And what do righteousness and being *without the Law* have in common? Or what fellowship can light have with darkness?

2 Thess. 2:3, 7:

> [3] Don't let anyone deceive you in any way, for that day will not come until falling away from God occurs and the man *without the Law* is revealed, the son of destruction. [7] And the secret power *without the Law* is already at work, but the one who now holds it back will be taken out of the way.

Titus 2:14:

> [14] who gave himself for us to redeem us from all deeds *without the Law* and to purify for himself a people that are his very own, eager to do what is good.

See Heb. 1:9:

> [9] You have loved righteousness and hated deeds *without the Law*; therefore God, your God, has set you above your companions by

anointing you with the oil of joy.

Heb. 8:12:

> [12] For I will forgive their wrongdoing, and I will never again remember their *violations of the Law*.

See Heb. 10:17:

> [17] And their sins and deeds *without the Law* I will remember no more.

2 Peter 2:8:

> [8] And that righteous man, living among them day after day, was tormented in his righteous soul by the deeds *without the Law* he saw and heard.

In the following *two* verses the translation was made correctly (Acts 23:3):

> [3] Then Paul said to him, "God will strike you, you whitewashed wall! And you sit there to judge me according to the Law, and you judge *without the Law* by commanding that I be struck!"

And in 1 Cor. 9:20-21:

> [20] And to the Jews I became like a Jew, to win the Jews. To those under the Law I became like one under the Law, as I myself am not under the Law, so as to win those under the Law. [21] To those *without the Law* I became like one *without the Law*, as I am not *without Law* before God, but am under the Law to Christ, so as to win those *without the Law*.

Those numerous examples are mentioned with the purpose of limiting counterarguments, such that the usage and misinterpretation of the word *anomos* are insignificant and may be omitted. The distinctive characteristics of the Antichrist in 2 Thess. 2:8-9 should not be mistranslated.

The Bible challenges readers with many inconspicuous "traps" which can lead to incorrect understandings. With the right preparation and knowledge, the traps may be avoided, but they are triggered if some-one has moved away from the correct message.

In cases where deviation from the text is further from the truth, the "noise" of incorrect translation increases the risk of entrapment.

The End of the Law

Proponents of Replacement Theology, which claims that the Church has replaced Israel and Jesus has annulled the Law, base their belief on the erroneous translation of Rom. 10:4:

> [4] For Christ is the *end of the law* for righteousness to everyone who believes.

They teach that all covenants God had made with Israel were passed down to the Church. According to the Bible, the Apostle Paul was never charged by his enemies for teaching the annulment of the Law of Moses.

Paul uses the Greek word *telos*, which bears multiple meanings. The most fitting central meaning is "supreme intention or inherent goal, the purpose of man's endeavor."[38] Thus we can retranslate:

> [4] For Christ is the *high point* of the Law for righteousness to every-one who believes.

In other words, the goal of the hundred-meter dash is not to stop run-ning, but to win an Olympic gold medal.

Moab Covenant

Moab Covenant is essential for understanding that the Church is a part of Israel and the New Covenant. This connection is far from being encouraged and recognized as a part of theology.

God commanded the strangers who sojourned in Israel and are willing to partake of Passover meal to go through the rite of conversion

---

38 An example found in Peter Enns Inspiration and Incarnation (2005) 125; Amy-Jill Levine, Marc Zvi Brettler, The Jewish Annotated New Testament (2017) 670.

(Ex. 12:48-49):

> [48] An alien living among you who wants to celebrate the Lord's Passover must have all the males in his household circumcised; then he may take part like one born in the land. No uncircumcised male may eat of it. [49] The same Law applies to the native-born and to the alien living among you.

The Moab Covenant was made in response to Israel's *infidelity* to God (Deut. 29:1):

> [1] These are the terms of the Covenant the Lord commanded Moses to make with the Israelites in Moab, *in addition* to the Covenant he had made with them at Horeb.

The Moab Covenant completes forty years of Israel's *punishment* in the wilderness.

God has made the *everlasting* Covenant, not only with Israel, but also with those Gentiles who were identified with Jews because of their faith, and with future generations of these two groups (Deut. 29:9-15):

> [9] Carefully follow the terms of this Covenant, so that you may prosper in everything you do. [10] All of you are standing today in the presence of the Lord your God, your leaders and chief men, your elders and officials, and all the other men of Israel, [11] together with your children and your wives, and the *aliens* living in your camps who chop your wood and carry your water. [12] You are standing here in order to enter into a Covenant with the Lord your God, a Covenant the Lord is making with you this day and sealing with an oath, [13] to confirm you this day as his people, that he may be your God as he promised you and as he swore to your fathers, Abraham, Isaac and Jacob. [14] I am making this Covenant, with its oath, not only with you [15] who are standing here with us today in the presence of the Lord our God but also with those who are not here today.

The Moab Covenant is made with four groups of people:

- Jews
- Gentiles who include themselves into Israel as believers in God of Abraham, Isaac and Jacob

- The descendants of those two groups
- Those who will join Israel in the future.

The fourth group includes Gentile Christians (Eph. 2:11-12, 19):

> [11] Therefore, remember that *formerly* you who are Gentiles in the flesh and called "uncircumcised" by those who call themselves "the circumcision" that done in the body by the hands of men [12] remember that at that time you were separate from Christ, excluded from citizenship in Israel and foreigners to the *Covenants* of the promise, without hope and without God in the world... [19] Consequently, you are *no longer* foreigners and aliens, but fellow citizens with God's people and members of God's household,

It is important that the *everlasting* Moab Covenant confirms the *everlasting* Covenants with Israel, the Law of Moses, and the Land Covenant. The Moab Covenant demonstrates how a Gentile may believe in God of Israel *without becoming a Jew.*

English-speaking Christians could read commentaries on the Moab Covenant in the works of John Gill in 1748, but the Moab Covenant is well known and studied in Judaism.[39] For forty years while wandering in the Sinai the people of Israel had to learn through experience the significance of obeying the commandments, both as individuals and as the nation. This Covenant is the one that binds later generations.

The words *karat habberit*, כָּרַת הַבְּרִית, and *likrot habberit*, translated as "cut the Covenant" (Deut. 29:1), are applied only to the time of giving the *new* Covenant, while *heqim berit* is used when God establishes an already given Covenant. Thus, the Moab Covenant was the new one made in addition to the Covenant with Israel. Any attempts to reduce the value of the Moab Covenant contradict the Bible. While promoters of Replacement Theology attempt to invalidate the Mosaic Covenant and the Law, the New Testament does not have a single verse against the Moab Covenant which *validates* the Covenant with Israel. The explanation of the importance of the Moab Covenant brings us to the realization that, if the Moab Covenant is excluded, Replacement Theology claims its space.

---

39 Haggai Ben-Arzi, The Covenant on the Plains of Moab.

Moab Covenant and New Covenant

Previous examples confirm that the Law of Moses is inextricably linked to the New Covenant. What is the basis for the inclusion of Gentiles in the New Covenant? The New Covenant is built upon the Moab Covenant. The Moab Covenant complements the Covenant with Israel. Consequently, the New Covenant evolved as being based on all previous Covenants.

Although God created his own nation, Israel, He foresaw the forth-coming acceptance of Gentiles sojourning among Israel and believing in Him (Gen. 17:23):

> [23] On that very day Abraham took his son Ishmael and all those born in his household or bought with his money, every male in his household, and circumcised them, as God told him.

Straightforward instructions are given in Gen. 17:10-13.

In the New Covenant the inclusion of Gentiles in Israel receives even more clarification (John 10:15-16):

> [15] Just as the Father knows me and I know the Father and I lay down my life for the sheep. [16] I have other sheep that are not of this fold. I must bring them also. They too will listen to my voice, and there shall be one flock and one shepherd.

Replacement Theology teaches that Gentile Christians supersede Jews as the people of God. Over the last two thousand years, attempts to create the new unified body of Jews and Gentiles have mostly failed. The comprehensive evidence is available in the book by James Parkes written in 1934 and based on his doctoral thesis completed two years earlier.[40]

Instead of reaffirming the Jewishness of Jesus, Replacement Theology completely focuses on Gentiles in the Church, and restricts Jews from joining the commonwealth.

The following verses were traditionally explained as a call to unity

---

40 James Parkes, The Conflict of the Church and Synagogue: A Study in the Origins of Anti-Sem-itism (1934).

among the different denominations which did not even exist in the time of Jesus. In the Bible, this unity is intended between Jews and Gentiles, and requires the presence of Jesus (John 17:20-23):

> [20] And my prayer is not for them alone. And I pray also for those who believe in me through their word, [21] that all of them may be one, Father, just as you are in me and I am in you. And may they also be in us so that the world may believe that you have sent me. [22] I have given them the glory that you gave me, that they may be one as we are one. [23] I in them and you in me. May they be brought to perfect in unity to let the world know that you sent me and have loved them as you have loved me.

Paul describes both the Moab Covenant and Gentile believers being brought into the commonwealth of Israel through their faith in and by Jesus (Eph. 2:11-15):

> [11] Therefore, remember that formerly you who are Gentiles by flesh and called "uncircumcised" by those who call themselves "the circumcision" that done in the body by the hands of men, [12] remember that at that time you were separate from Christ, excluded from citizenship in Israel and aliens to the Covenants of the promise, without hope and without God in the world. [13] And now in Christ Jesus you who once were far away have been brought near through the blood of Christ. [14] And he himself is our peace, who has made the two one and has *untied* the barrier, the dividing wall of hostility, [15] by abolishing in his flesh the Law with its commandments and regulations. His purpose was to create in himself one new man out of the two, thus making peace.

It could only be the wall in the Temple separating the court of the Gentiles from the rest of the Temple for Paul in v. 14. This is also indicated by the word *untie* or *loose*, which has Hebrew meaning of permitting or allowing. In this context Paul calls the union of Jews and Gentiles in one body.

If the barrier between Jews and Gentile believers no longer exists, then the logical conclusion would be found in Eph. 2:19-21:

> [19] Consequently, you are no longer foreigners and aliens, but fellow

citizens with God's people and members of God's household, [20]built on the foundation of the apostles and prophets, with Christ Jesus himself as the chief cornerstone. [21] In him the whole building is joined together and rises to become a holy Temple in the Lord.

See also Eph. 3:4-6:

[4] In reading this you will be able to understand my insight into the mystery of Christ, [5] which was not made known to men in other generations as it has now been revealed by the Spirit to God's holy apostles and prophets. [6] This mystery is that the Gentiles are heirs together with Israel, members together of one body, and sharers together in the promise in Christ Jesus through the gospel.

Paul elaborates on the purpose and meaning of the union in Rom. 11:11-12, 17-30:

[11] And I say then: Did they stumble as to fall? Not at all! Rather, because of their trespass, salvation has come to the Gentiles to make them [Jews] envious. [12] But if their trespass means riches for the world, and their loss means riches for the Gentiles, how much greater riches will their fullness bring!...
[17] And if some of the branches have been broken off, and you, though a wild olive shoot, have been grafted in among the others and now share in the nourishing sap from the olive root, [18] do not be arrogant over those branches. If you do, consider this: You do not support the root, but the root supports you. [19] You will say then, "Branches were broken off so that I could be grafted in." [20]Granted, they were broken off because of unbelief, and you stand by faith. Do not be proud, but fear. [21] And if God did not spare the natural branches, he will not spare you either. [22] And consider therefore the kindness and sternness of God: sternness to those who fell, and kindness to you, provided that you continue in his kindness. And otherwise, you also will be cut off. [23] And if they [Jews] do not persist in unbelief, they will be grafted in, for God is able to graft them in again. [24] And if you were cut out of an olive tree that is wild by nature, and contrary to nature were grafted into a cultivated olive tree, how much more readily will these, the natural branches, be grafted into their own olive tree! [25] And I do not

want you to be ignorant of this mystery, brothers, so that you may not be conceited: Israel has experienced a hardening in part until the full number of the Gentiles has come in. [26] And so all Israel will be saved, as it is written: "The deliverer will come from Zion; he will turn godlessness away from Jacob. [27] And this is my Covenant with them when I take away their sins. [28] As far as the gospel is concerned they are enemies on your account, and as far as election is concerned, they are loved on account of the forefathers, [29] and God's gifts and his call are irrevocable. [30] And just as you who were at one time disobedient to God have now received mercy as a result of their disobedience, [31] and so they too have now become disobedient in order that they too may now receive mercy through God's mercy to you.

For Paul the existence of Gentile believers in the Church serves the purpose of bringing all Jews to the faith in their Messiah.

New Covenant

An important scriptural passage on Covenants can be found in Jer. 31:31-33:

> [31] I will make a new Covenant with the house of Israel and with the house of Judah. [32] It will not be like the Covenant I made with their forefathers when I took them by the hand to lead them out of Egypt, because they broke my Covenant, though I was a husband to them, declares the Lord. [33] This is the Covenant I will make with the house of Israel, declares the Lord. I will put my Law in their minds and write it on their hearts, and I will be their God, and they will be my people.

The verses highlight the following:

- Israel once again broke the Mosaic Covenant
- God responds to the Covenant's breaking with the giving of another Covenant
- The New Covenant is *promised to Israel*
- The New Covenant *confirms the* promise of the Mosaic Covenant: "I will be their God, and they will be my people."

The first time we read about the New Covenant in the New Testament in Luke 22:19-20:

> [19] And he took bread, gave thanks and broke it, and gave it to them, saying, "This is my body given for you; do this in remembrance of me." [20] And in the same way, after the supper he took the cup, saying, "This cup is the *New Covenant* in my blood, which is poured out for you."

According to the Biblical narrative, Jesus instituted the observance of communion, which is kept by all Christians. Therefore, it is reasonable to presume that the first *ecclesia* of the New Covenant was born at that time.

We have all heard the teaching that the Church was born when the disciples received the Holy Spirit on the day of Pentecost, *Shavuot* in Hebrew, as described in Acts 2. However, the Holy Spirit was given to His disciples earlier, on the day of Jesus' resurrection (John 20:19-23):

> [19] And on the evening of that first day of the week, and where the disciples were together, with the doors locked for fear of the Jews, Jesus came and stood among them and said, "*Shalom aleichem!*" [20] And after he said this, he showed them his hands and side. And the disciples were overjoyed when they saw the Lord. [21] And again Jesus said, "Peace be with you! As the Father has sent me, I am sending you." [22] And with that he *breathed* on them and said, "*Receive the Holy Spirit.* [23] If you forgive anyone his sins, they are forgiven; if you withhold them, it is withheld."

Communion was received on the day of the crucifixion (in the Jewish calendar, the day begins at sunset) and the Holy Spirit was received by disciples on the day of Jesus' resurrection.[41] They were also given the authority to forgive sins on that day.

When the disciples received the Holy Spirit, they were born from above. This brings us to Gen. 2:7:

> [7] The Lord God formed the man from the dust of the ground and

---

41 The Lord was crucified on Friday and resurrected on Sunday.

breathed into his nostrils the breath of life, and the man became a living being.

Jesus imparting the Holy Spirit is as profound as the creation of humanity and resurrection being connected as well.

Chronologically, Jesus creates the first communion at the feast of Passover (Matt. 26:26-27):

> [26] As they were eating, Jesus took bread, blessed and broke it, gave it to the disciples, and said, "Take and eat it; this is my body." [27] Then he took a cup, and after giving thanks, he gave it to them and said, "Drink from it, all of you.

Before partaking, *bracha rishona* (food fore-blessings) were said: "Blessed are You, Lord our God, King of the Universe, Who brings forth bread from the earth, and blessed are You, Lord our God, King of the Universe, Who creates *the fruit of the vine.*" That is why we read in Matt. 26:29:

> [29] But I tell you, I will not drink from this *fruit of the vine* until the kingdom of God comes.

This is the literal translation from Hebrew.

The very early development of the First Church took place in the presence of the living Lord (Acts 1:2-3):

> [2] ...he was taken up to heaven, after giving instructions through the Holy Spirit to the apostles he had chosen. [3] After his suffering, he showed himself to these men and gave many convincing proofs that he was alive. He appeared to them over a period of forty days and spoke about the kingdom of God.

Luke supported the idea that the Church was not born in the first century, but it existed before, when Israel was wandering in the wilderness (Acts 7:37-38):

> [37] This is that Moses who told the Israelites, "God will send you a prophet like me from your own people. [38] He was in the *ecclesia* in the desert, with the angel who spoke to him on Mount Sinai, and

with our fathers; and he received living words to pass on to us."

Those living words represent the Covenant with Israel and the commandments of the Law of Moses. They point out that the Church, or *ecclesia*, already existed even before receiving the Law (Ex. 19-20); a gathering of believers in God took place.

Most commentaries state that Covenants are built on each other, with the single exception of the New Covenant, which replaced the Covenant with Israel. The critical verse for that "conclusion" is quoted out of context from Heb. 8:13:

> [13] By calling this covenant "new," he has made the first one obsolete; and what is obsolete and aging will soon disappear.

A better translation can be found in the context of Heb. 8:8, 10, 13:

> [8] But God found fault with the people and said: "The time is coming, declares the Lord, when I will make a new covenant with the house of Israel and with the house of Judah...
> [10] This is the covenant I will make with the house of Israel after that time, declares the Lord...
> [13] By calling [this covenant] "new," he has made the first one old, and what is growing old, and aging, near disappearance.

Thus, the author of the Letter to the Hebrews reasons using Jer. 31:31-34 by calling this Covenant "new." Jeremiah does not renounce the old Covenant. The New Covenant is perfect, complete and ratified with the blood of the Messiah.

First, the Covenant with Israel is *everlasting*. The Bible does not support the reclassification which claims that the Covenant with Israel is *temporary*. Second, the Letter to the Hebrews explicitly states that the New Covenant has been made with the house of Israel and the house of Judah. Third, God found fault not with the Covenant with Israel, but with the people of Israel.

The question is what would be "near disappearance" in the time when the Letter was written? The answer comes from the next verses (Heb. 9:1, 2). The word "and" as the common conjunction in the beginning of the phrase confirms that the following sentence continues the previous one. All translations misrepresent the text by adding meaning which is not in the original text; for example, in the NIV version:

> 9:1 Now the first covenant had regulations for worship and also an earthly sanctuary. 2 A tabernacle was set up.

The correct translation should be:

> 9:1 And indeed and the first had regulations of worship and the *earthly sanctuary*. 2 And the *tabernacle* was set up...

Hebrews 8 describes sacrifices of the priests with a present-tense verb, referring to the Temple, which is destined to be destroyed by Romans in a few months. The part of the Mosaic Law regarding the Temple service would cease to be practiced.[42]

Israel's spiritual redemption and restoration will be complete upon Jesus' second coming (Rom. 11:26). Being the Messiah of Israel, Jesus is the fulfillment of her destiny.

There was a critical development of the character of the Church at the first Council of Nicaea in 325. The agenda of the Synod, convoked by the Roman Emperor Constantine, included the discussion on the celebration of Passover. Later, Constantine wrote: "Let us have nothing to do with the *detestable* Jewish rabble (Sabbath)" and "Therefore we have nothing in common with that most hostile people, the Jews. We have received *another* way from the Savior."[43] Shortly after that all Jewish festivals and customs faded out from Church practice.

Jesus in the Old Testament

Despite some claims that Jesus is the God of the New Testament only, we read in John 1:1-3:

> 1:1 In the beginning was the Word, and the Word was with God, and the Word was God. 2 He was with God in the beginning. 3 Through

---

42 Kaiser, W. C., Jr. Recovering the Unity of the Bible (2009) 157, 168; Craig S. Keener, Bible Background Commentary, New Testament (1993) 665-666.

43 Eusebius Pamphilus, Eusebius' Ecclesiastical History 423.

him all things were made; without him nothing was made that has been made.

Thus, the New Testament teaches otherwise. Jesus created the entire universe. The Lord's own words clarify the timing (John 8:56-58):

> [56] Your father Abraham rejoiced at the thought of seeing my day; and he saw it and was glad." [57] And the Jews said to him, "you are not yet fifty years old, and you have seen Abraham?" [58] Jesus said to them, "I tell you the truth, before Abraham was born, I am!"

Paul confirms His status as God of the Old and New Testaments (Col. 1:16-17):

> [16] For by him all things were created: things in heaven and on earth, visible and invisible, whether thrones or powers or rulers or authorities; all things were created by him and for him. [17] And He is before all things, and in him all things hold together.

Jesus became the sustenance and their spiritual food and drink while leading the people of Israel, *including believing Gentiles*, in the wilderness (1 Cor. 10:1-4, 9):

> [1] And I do not want you to be ignorant, brothers, that our forefathers were all under the cloud and that they all passed through the sea. [2] And they were all baptized into Moses in the cloud and in the sea. [3] And they all ate the same spiritual food [4] and drank the same spiritual drink; and they drank from the spiritual rock that followed them, and that rock was Christ...
> [9] And we should not test the Christ, as some of them did, and were killed by snakes.

Paul uses *gezera shava* while quoting Neh. 9:11-16, where the prophet summarized the critical events of the Exodus.

According to the words of the anonymous author Moses chose disgrace for the sake of Christ in the time when he could have lived in splendor and opulence (Heb. 11:24-26):

> [24] By faith Moses, when he had grown up, refused to be known as the son of Pharaoh's daughter. [25] He chose to be mistreated along

with the people of God rather than to enjoy the fleeting pleasures of sin. [26] He considered the reproach of Christ greater wealth than the treasures of Egypt, and he was looking to his reward.

Difficulties in Bible Translation

Biblical Language

God's infallible word is not easy to read and discern. The Old Testament is written in Hebrew, with the following texts in Aramaic: Dan. 2:4-7:28; Ezra 4:8-6:18, 7:12-26; Jer. 10:11. A few words in the New Testament are identified as Aramaic: Abba, Eloi, Kepha, Tabitha, Maranatha, bar (son of).

The Biblical books were written over the course of more than a thousand years, and during this time language changed, being influenced by other languages of either neighboring nations or conquerors.

The Old Testament provides an essential context for understanding the way in which the New Testament has been shaped. When the student of the Bible learns how first-century Judaism operated, there will be no misunderstanding what Jesus is talking about.

New Testament language is more uniform than the Old, though it is the case that each New Testament book is written in its own way, and the reader can easily distinguish between authors.

In all likelihood, only the Letter to the Hebrews was written by a native Greek speaker; all other New Testament texts were written by native Hebrew speakers while Greek was the foreign language. Using an Interlinear Bible allows us to study these subtle differences on a deeper level.

The New Testament's Greek prose lacks much of the subtlety of classical Greek. Greek in the New Testament is characterized by simplified verb syntax, less involved syntax, an increased frequency of prepositions and compound verbs, and a tendency to disregard the rules of concord.[44]

Lost in Translation

I will now review a few cases where the English translation of the Greek New Testament text needs correction.

Are we saved by our own faith in Jesus or through faith of Jesus?

Most Bible versions mistranslate Rom. 3:22 by changing the words "faith of Jesus" to "faith in Jesus." The Greek text states:

> [22] This righteousness from God comes through faith *of* Jesus Christ to all who believe. There is no difference...

The Greek text uses the *genitive masculine* case for the noun. The traditional translation "in Jesus" corresponds to the *dative* case. Paul repeats this idea in Gal. 2:16:

> [16] ...know that a man is not justified by observing the law, but by faith *of* Jesus Christ.

The original Greek text states that faith comes from the Lord Jesus, but the translations redirect the message to human faith (Gal. 3:22):

> [22] But the Scripture declares that the whole world is a prisoner of sin, so that what was promised, being given through faith *of* Jesus Christ, might be given to those who believe.

Eph. 3:12:

> [12] In him and through faith *from* Him we may approach God with freedom and confidence.

Phil. 3:9:

> [9] ...and be found in him, not having a righteousness of my own that comes from the law, but that which is through faith *from* Christ:

---

44 David Hill, Some important soteriological terms In the New Testament: a study in semantics. PhD thesis (1964) 18-19.

the righteousness that comes from God and is by faith.

The Greek words for Christ (*Christou*) and God (*Theou*) in Phil. 3:9 are used in the *genitive* masculine case as well.

Another case of "lost in translation" is John 1:11:

> [11] He came to that which was his *own*, but his *own* did not receive him.

While the same English word is repeated, in Greek "own" represents two *different* words. The first "own" is in *neuter* gender, while the second "own" is *masculine*. Those who have not received Jesus do not belong to the same group as the one which the Messiah has come to. Additionally, Apostle John used exaggerations for emphasis and brought together quite different groups of people. A more accurate statement would be:

> [11] He came to that which was his own [all Israel], but His own [unbelieving Jews] did not receive Him.

See Ps. 119:29 (NIV):

> [29] Keep me from deceitful ways; be gracious to me through your law.

This verse in Hebrew reads: *Dereko sheker haser mimmenni, v'torateka chaneni*. The word "way," *dereko*, is singular, and it means a person's wrongful behavior. The word *chaneni* is about showing favor. The word *v'torateka* does not mean a law; the word "Torah" connotates the Law, or the first five books of the Bible, and Jews understand it as instructions or directions. The Christian Standard Bible version is closer to the text:

> [29] Keep me from the way of deceit and graciously give me your instruction.

A better translation would be:

> [29] Keep me from the *way of falsehood* and *benevolently* give me your *guidance*.

The "And" Conjunction

An important feature of the Hebrew as well as other Semitic languages is *parataxis*. The sentences connected via the "and" conjunction may be compared with a chain of elephants, where each one holds the tail of its companion. The reader recognizes that the narrative which has started in the previous sentence is not complete yet. Indo-European languages, like English or Greek, are based on another structure: *hypotaxis*, which allows one to build complex sentences.

The authors of the New Testament books had their thinking process filled with *parataxis* but had to write in *hypotaxis*.

One recognizes the structure of the *parataxis* by the conjunction "and," which is often located in the beginning of a phrase. It shows the logical connection between sentences and gives a certain rhythm to the narrative called rhythmic prose in Hebrew. That is why Psalms are so melodic and amenable to singing.

The outcome demonstrates that the reasoning is not complete. Thus, the phrase should be read in the context of the previous one.

Hebrew, unlike European languages, uses "and" as a prefix to a verb where it sounds like "v" or "u." In the Adon Olam prayer, for example, one will recite: *V'hu hayah v'hu hoveh v'hu yihyeh betifarah* (and He was, and He is, and He will be, into glorious eternity). This is based on God's self-identification in Ex. 3:14, "I am who I am," or "I will be who I will be." We can see similar syntax in Rom. 9:4:

> [4] They are Israelites, *and* to them belong the adoption, *and* the glory, *and* the covenants, *and* the giving of the Law, *and* the Temple service, *and* the promises.

All conjunctions in Greek (δέ, καί, *oun, gar,* ἄρα, *men, te, alla, dio, tote, hōste*) are united with the same equivalent of *vav* in Hebrew.

The word Ἐγένετο, "it came to pass" in KJV, which is used widely in the Gospels, is a translation of the Hebrew word *hayah*, "it was." This Semitism is used far more frequently in Luke's writings than elsewhere (see Luke 1:5, 1:8, 1:23, 1:41, 1:44, 1:59, 1:65, 2:1, 2:6, 2:15,

3:21, 5:1, 5:12, 5:17, 6:1, 6:6, 6:12, 7:11, 8:1, 8:22, 9:18, 9:28,9:37, 9:51, 11:1, 11:27, 14:1, 17:11, 18:35, 20:1, 22:24, 24:4).

The structure of *parataxis* presents the narrative of Luke 1:

[1] Forasmuch as many have taken in hand to set forth in order a declaration of those things which are most surely believed among us, [2]Even as they delivered them unto us, which from the beginning were eyewitnesses, *and* ministers of the word; [3] It seemed good to me also, having had perfect understanding of all things from the very first, to write unto thee in order, most excellent Theophilus, [4]That thou mightest know the certainty of those things, wherein thou hast been instructed. [5] It came to pass in the days of Herod, the king of Judaea, a certain priest named Zacharias, of the course of Abia: *and* his wife *was* of the daughters of Aaron, *and* her name *was* Elisabeth. [6]*And* they were both righteous before God, walking in all the commandments *and* ordinances of the Lord blameless. [7]*And* they had no child, because that Elisabeth was barren, *and* they both were *now* well stricken in years. [8]*And* it came to pass, that while he executed the priest's office before God in the order of his course, [9]According to the custom of the priest's office, his lot was to burn incense when he went into the temple of the Lord. [10]*And* the whole multitude of the people were praying without at the time of incense. [11]*And* there appeared unto him an angel of the Lord standing on the right side of the altar of incense. [12]*And* when Zacharias saw *him*, he was troubled, **and** fear fell upon him. [13]*And* the angel said unto him, Fear not, Zacharias: for thy prayer is heard; *and* thy wife Elisabeth shall bear thee a son, *and* thou shalt call his name John. [14]*And* thou shalt have joy *and* gladness; *and* many shall rejoice at his birth. [15]*And* he shall be great in the sight of the Lord, *and* shall drink neither wine **and** nor strong drink; *and* he shall be filled with the Holy Ghost, even from his mother's womb. [16]*And* many of the children of Israel shall he turn to the Lord their God. [17]*And* he shall go before him in the spirit and power of Elias, to turn the hearts of the fathers to the children, *and* the disobedient to the wisdom of the just; *and* to make ready a people prepared for the Lord. [18]*And* Zacharias said unto the angel: Whereby shall I know this? *And* I am an old man, *and* my wife well stricken in years. [19]*And* the angel answering said unto him, I

am Gabriel that stand in the presence of God; *and* am sent to speak unto thee, *and* to shew thee these glad tidings. ²⁰ *And*, behold, thou shalt be dumb, *and* not able to speak, until the day that these things shall be performed, because thou believest not my words, which shall be fulfilled in their season. ²¹ *And* the people waited for Zacharias, *and* marveled that he tarried so long in the temple. ²² *And* when he came out, he could not speak unto them: *and* they perceived that he had seen a vision in the temple: *and* he beckoned unto them, *and* remained speechless. ²³ *And* it came to pass, that, as soon as the days of his ministration were accomplished, he departed to his own house. ²⁴ *And* after those days his wife Elisabeth conceived, *and* hid herself five months, saying, ²⁵ Thus hath the Lord dealt with me in the days wherein he looked on *me*, to take away my reproach among men. ²⁶ *And* in the sixth month the angel Gabriel was sent from God unto a city of Galilee, named Nazareth, ²⁷ To a virgin espoused to a man whose name was Joseph, of the house of David; *and* the virgin's name *was* Mariam. ²⁸ *And* the angel came in unto her, and said, Hail, *thou that art* highly favoured, the Lord *is* with thee: blessed *art* thou among women. ²⁹ *And* when she saw *him*, she was troubled at his saying, *and* cast in her mind what manner of salutation this should be. ³⁰ *And* the angel said unto her, Fear not, Mariam: *and* thou hast found favour with God. ³¹ *And*, behold, thou shalt conceive in thy womb, *and* bring forth a son, *and* shalt call his name JESUS. ³² He shall be great, *and* shall be called the Son of the Highest: *and* the Lord God shall give unto him the throne of his father David: ³³ *And* he shall reign over the house of Jacob forever; *and* of his kingdom there shall be no end. ³⁴ *And* Mariam said unto the angel, How shall this be, seeing I know not a man? ³⁵ *And* the angel answered and said unto her, The Holy Ghost shall come upon thee, *and* the power of the Highest shall overshadow thee: *and* that holy thing which shall be born of thee shall be called the Son of God. ³⁶ *And*, behold, thy cousin Elisabeth, *and* she hath also conceived a son in her old age: *and* this is the sixth month with her, who was called barren. ³⁷ For with God nothing shall be impossible. ³⁸ *And* Mariam said, Behold the handmaid of the Lord; be it unto me according to thy word. *And* the angel departed from her. ³⁹ *And* Mariam arose in those days, *and* went into the hill country with haste, into a city of Juda;

[40] *And* entered into the house of Zacharias, *and* saluted Elisabeth. [41] *And* it came to pass, that, when Elisabeth heard the salutation of Mariam, the babe leaped in her womb; *and* Elisabeth was filled with the Holy Ghost: [42] *And* she spake out with a loud voice, *and* said, Blessed *art* thou among women, *and* blessed *is* the fruit of thy womb. [43] *And* whence *is* this to me that the mother of my Lord should come to me? [44] *And* as came to pass the voice of thy salutation sounded in mine ears, the babe leaped in my womb for joy. [45] *And* blessed *is* she that believed: for there shall be a performance of those things which were told her from the Lord. [46] *And* Mariam said: My soul doth magnify the Lord, [47] *And* my spirit hath rejoiced in God my Saviour. [48] For he *hath* regarded the low estate of his handmaiden: *and*, behold, from henceforth all generations shall call me blessed. [49] For he that is mighty hath done to me great things; *and* holy *is* his name. [50] *And* his mercy *is* on them *and* fear him from generation to generation. [51] He hath shewed strength with his arm; he hath scattered the proud in the imagination of their hearts. [52] He hath put down the mighty from *their* seats, **and** exalted them of low degree. [53] He hath filled the hungry with good things; *and* the rich he hath sent empty away. [54] He hath holpen his servant Israel, in remembrance of *his* mercy; [55] As he spake to our fathers, to Abraham, *and* to his seed forever. [56] *And* Mariam abode with her about three months, *and* returned to her own house. [57] *And* Elisabeth's full time came that she should be delivered; *and* she brought forth a son. [58] *And* her neighbors *and* her cousins heard how the Lord had shewed great mercy upon her; *and* they rejoiced with her. [59] *And* it came to pass, that on the eighth day they came to circumcise the child; *and* they called him Zacharias, after the name of his father. [60] *And* his mother answered and said, Not *so*; but he shall be called John. [61] *And* they said unto her, There is none of thy kindred that is called by this name. [62] *And* they made signs to his father, how he would have him called. [63] *And* he asked for a writing table, *and* wrote, saying, His name is John. *And* they marveled all. [64] *And* his mouth was opened immediately, *and* his tongue *loosed*, *and* he spake, and praised God. [65] *And* it came to pass fear on all that dwelt round about them: *and* all these sayings were noised abroad throughout all the hill country of Judaea. [66] *And* all they that heard *them* laid *them* up in their hearts, saying, What

manner of child shall this be! *And* the hand of the Lord was with him. [67] *And* his father Zacharias was filled with the Holy Ghost, **and** prophesied, saying, [68] Blessed *be* the Lord God of Israel; for he hath visited *and* redeemed his people, [69] *And* hath raised up an horn of salvation for us in the house of his servant David; [70] As he spake by the mouth of his holy prophets, which have been since the world began: [71] That we should be saved from our enemies, *and* from the hand of all that hate us; [72] To perform the mercy *promised* to our fathers, *and* to remember his holy covenant; [73] The oath which he sware to our father Abraham, [74] That he would grant unto us, that we being delivered out of the hand of our enemies might serve him without fear, [75] In holiness *and* righteousness before him, all the days of our life. [76] *And* thou, *and* child, shalt be called the prophet of the Highest: *and* thou shalt go before the face of the Lord to prepare his ways; [77] To give knowledge of salvation unto his people by the remission of their sins, [78] Through the tender mercy of our God; whereby the dayspring from on high hath visited us, [79] To give light to them that sit in darkness **and** *in* the shadow of death, to guide our feet into the way of peace. [80] *And* the child grew, *and* waxed strong in spirit, *and* was in the deserts till the day of his shewing unto Israel.

The frequency of the word "and," the conjunctive vav in Hebrew, in this chapter is 7.5%, which is drastically different from the 1% frequency typical for Greek prose. Notably, Luke 2 through 11 also begins with the "and" conjunction.

Luke's usage of Greek conjunctions closely relates to the language of the Septuagint. See, for example Gen. 1:1-5:

Ἐν ἀρχῇ ἐποίησεν ὁ θεὸς τὸν οὐρανὸν **καὶ** τὴν γῆν. 2 ἡ **δὲ** γῆ ἦν ἀόρατος **καὶ** ἀκατασκεύαστος, **καὶ** σκότος ἐπάνω τῆς ἀβύσσου, **καὶ** πνεῦμα θεοῦ ἐπεφέρετο ἐπάνω τοῦ ὕδατος. 3 **καὶ** εἶπεν ὁ θεός Γενηθήτω φῶς. **καὶ** **ἐγένετο** φῶς. 4 **καὶ** εἶδεν ὁ θεὸς τὸ φῶς ὅτι καλόν. **καὶ** διεχώρισεν ὁ θεὸς ἀνὰ μέσον τοῦ φωτὸς **καὶ** ἀνὰ μέσον τοῦ σκότους. 5 **καὶ** ἐκάλεσεν ὁ θεὸς τὸ φῶς ἡμέραν **καὶ** τὸ σκότος ἐκάλεσεν νύκτα. **καὶ** **ἐγένετο** ἑσπέρα **καὶ** **ἐγένετο** πρωΐ, ἡμέρα μία.

Those verses have thirteen conjunctions which comprise 15.7% of the text, approximately twice as high as the typical passage in the Septuagint.

Is it justified to include this conjunction with the purpose of giving a clear sense of a foreign language? This is precisely the way that Luke's Gospel was heard by his listeners at the time. Textual analysis shows that the entire Bible, from the first to the last line, was written by Hebrew-speaking men.[45]

Septuagint

First-century believers outside Israel had the Old Testament in Greek; the Septuagint is not exactly a word-for-word translation, as it differs in some cases from the Hebrew original and sometimes presents an exegesis of the Hebrew text. Here is an example of a significant difference (Matt. 1:23):

> [23] Behold, the *virgin* shall conceive and bear a son, and they shall call his name Immanuel which means, God with us.

Compare the quotation from Isa. 7:14 (LXX[46]) with the Hebrew text:

> [14] The Lord himself will give you a sign. Behold, the *maiden* shall conceive and bear a son, and shall call his name Immanuel.

Matthew did not invent anything, but merely cited the text from the Septuagint. More than half of the quotations from the Old Testament in the New Testament are given not from original Hebrew, but from the Septuagint. There are many commentaries which state that the Hebrew word *alma* should be translated as "a young female," but in the Septuagint it was translated by the word "virgin," *parthenos*, which has no other meaning.[47] The translators of the Septuagint obviously had

---

45 Some examples of Hebraisms in the New Testaments are in W. Leonard Grant, Hebrew, Aramaic, and the Greek of the Gospels, Greece & Rome, Vol. 20, No. 60 (Oct., 1951), 115-122; Randall Buth, R.Steven Notley The Language Environment of First Century Judaea (2014).

46 LXX – abbreviation of Septuagint's name.

47 For more on this subject, see Amy-Jill Levine and Marc Zvi Brettler, *The Bible With and Without Jesus: How Jews and Christians Read the Same Stories Differently* (2020), 240-66.

knowledge of Jewish Scriptures and translation skills.

The word Septuagint is Latin for "seventy." In roughly the third century B.C., Greek became the everyday language of Jews in Egyptian Alexandria. Although the entire liturgy was still conducted in Hebrew, Greek became their native language. The problem was that Egyptian believers in God of Israel did not know Hebrew and needed the Bible translated into their language; thus, the Pentateuch was translated into Greek. According to the legend, seventy elders, experts in the language, were engaged in it, each in a separate room. Upon comparing the translations agreed in every detail, which qualifies as embellishment to the legend. Another variant states that there were seventy-two translators, but two of them died before they completed the mission.

Modern linguists affirm that the translation was made by Alexandrian Jews, and that there were no fewer than three and no more than six of them. The rest of the books of the Bible were translated over the next two hundred years, and the quality of their translations significantly varied. The Book of Daniel was half the length of the version in the modern Bible and was replaced by Theodot's translation. The LXX Book of Esther is longer than the version found in the Hebrew Bible. Deuterocanonical and Apocryphal books were added to the Septuagint later on, and the widely known legend of the Septuagint's origin was born in the fictional letter of Aristeas to Philocrates,[48] written in 127-118 B.C. for propaganda purposes.

Judaism treated the Septuagint negatively after the development of anti-Jewish teachings in early Christianity. In the present day, it is considered a Gentile Christian book rather than proper translation of the Scriptures.

Tenses in Hebrew

In Biblical Hebrew, the order of words is different from English: verb-subject-object, as the verb carries most of the message. Most words are three-consonant clusters without vowels, which may include verbs and nouns. Besides, there are plenty of homonyms, words with

---

48 The letter of Aristeas, 1904.

different meanings and origins but with the same spelling. When a quotation is placed in a new context, then its meaning may be changed, and it becomes especially difficult to trace an author's thoughts upon translation into the Greek, as it is nearly impossible to trace homonyms in the original text the way the author intends.

The verb's prefixes define the active or passive voice, the male or female gender of the object of action. In addition, the prefix defines the connection with previous sentence. All is valid for the perfective aspect. For the imperfective aspect, some of these functions are moved to a suffix, though there are always exceptions to this rule.

The Biblical Hebrew does not have tenses. It has aspects instead. An aspect is a simple action, whether it is completed or not. Thus, Hebrew requires to specify the time of the action. See an example in Luke 1:5:

> 5 It came to pass *in the days of Herod*, king of Judea, there was a certain priest named Zacharias, of the division of Abijah; and he had a wife from the daughters of Aaron, and her name was Elizabeth.

Therefore, the understanding of the action's completeness depends on the context, and sometimes the context changes the time when that action takes place. For example, what took place in the past may transit to the future, or present, or even to a different past. In addition, the meaning of the verb in the new context may also be altered.

Modern Hebrew contains a much greater vocabulary, three grammar tenses, simplified pronunciation, a different order of words, and a different alphabet.

The Hebrew language bears the imprint of a Jewish mind. All Semitic people understand the concept of time a little bit differently than Europeans. They do not feel that any timeframe may be separate from "now," or refer to a "long time ago," or have the idea of "forgive and forget." Instead, Semitic people speak of yesterday, today, and tomorrow, which are necessarily relevant for "right now."

The Hebraic Mindset

The Hebraic mindset is of a Biblical faith-driven nature. It was the mindset of Jesus and His disciples. To better understand the New Testament, one should strive to reason "in Hebrew." Paul writes in 2 Cor. 5:21:

> [21] And he who knew no sin made sin [sacrifice for sin], for us, that we might have the righteousness of God in him.

Let's analyze whether Jesus became the curse in Gal. 3:13-14:

> [13] Christ redeemed us from the curse of the Law by becoming a *curse* [redeemer of curse] for us, for it is written: "Cursed is everyone who is hung on a tree." [14] He redeemed us in order that the blessing given to Abraham might come to the Gentiles through Christ Jesus, so that through faith we might receive the promise of the Spirit.

Some commentaries either avoid the subject or explain that Jesus somehow has sinned and become cursed. However, the Hebrew word "sin" may be the abbreviation of "sin-offering," as it is common in the Talmud, or it may refer to "atonement for a sin."[49] The same applies to the related word "curse." The single word with many meanings in Hebrew may be translated by a few words in Greek. Otherwise, it might be understood that there exists some righteousness "from sin," and Jesus became sin and curse, which is impossible.

The curse of the Law is the curse for intentional noncompliance with the commandments: the natural state of pagans. Gentile believers in the God of Abraham, Isaac, and Jacob become descendants of Abraham and recipients of Abraham's blessings. Most importantly, they become *righteous believers*.

The verses from the Letter to the Galatians are correlated with the text of Deut. 21:22-23 (LXX) by rule *gezera shava*:

> [22] And if there be sin in any with the judgment of death upon him

---

49 Johann Peter Lange, Theological and Homiletical Commentary on the Gospel of St-Matthew (1863), 2:418.

and he should die, and you should hang him upon a tree, [23] his body shall not rest upon the tree, but by burial you shall entomb him on that day for being cursed by God is every one hanging upon a tree, and in no way shall you defile the land.

Both texts describe the convicted person hanging on a tree (the main characteristic) and the redemption of guilt (the secondary characteristic). The first text can also be "extended" to the second. The choice of the main and secondary characteristics is subjective.

Paul taught that Jesus became a *sacrifice of atonement* for a sin. He is the curse's *atonement* for unbelievers as well, rather than the curse.

Dates of the New Testament Books

Since there were no records of publication at that time, it is necessary to resort to indirect methods to determine the chronology of New Testament texts, which are full of uncertainties. While some books can be dated more or less precisely, many cannot be. The chronological listing does not follow the arrangement in the New Testament; it should be taken into account that early books cannot refer to the books written later.

Approximate dates are as follows:

51 — 1 Thessalonians
52 — 2 Thessalonians
53 — Galatians
55 — 1 Corinthians
55 — 2 Corinthians
58 — Romans
60 — Ephesians
60 — Colossians
60 — Philemon
60-64 — 1 Peter
61 — Philippians
62 — James
63 — Titus
63-65 —1 Timothy

64 — Mark
65 — Jude
65-68 — 2 Peter
67 — 2 Timothy
70 — Matthew
70 — Hebrews
70 — Luke
70 — Acts
85-95 — 1 John
85-95 — 2 John
85-95 — 3 John
90 — John
95 — Revelation
115 — Both endings of Mark's Gospel

Chronological Bible

Creating a chronological order for these texts fails to present a true picture of Jesus' life. For the most part, the events do fit into a coherent picture, but a very caustic assessment of the "success" of such attempts was given more than a hundred and fifty years ago.[50] Some of the basic difficulties for harmonizing the Gospels chronologically can be traced to the lack of knowledge of the nature of the New Testament books.

For example, consider the text which describes two events: the withered fig tree and the casting out of money-changers from the Temple (Mark 11:12-21; Matt. 21:12-19).

In Matthew's Gospel, Jesus goes to Jerusalem, sees the fig tree, curses it, the tree immediately dries up, and then Jesus casts out money-changers from the Temple.

In the Gospel of Mark, Jesus goes to Jerusalem, sees the fig tree, curses it, goes to the Temple, throws out the money-changers, and the next day goes up to Jerusalem and sees the withered fig tree.

In Mark's Gospel, the story of the fig tree *frames* the story of the Temple as the prophecy: the fate of the fig tree also awaits the Temple.

---

50 Richard Watson, An exposition of the gospels of St. Matthew and St. Mark (1852) 16.

The prophecy comes at the time when the fall of Jerusalem and the destruction of the Temple seemed implausible.

In Matthew's Gospel, the story of the fig tree *follows* the story of the Temple and serves as a *hint* that the Temple will soon suffer the fate of the fig tree. The prophecy was given in the last year of the siege of Jerusalem, when the destruction of the Temple was a matter of the near future, and the hearers of the Gospel only needed a hint.

Both Gospels draw the same outcome; they simply do it in different ways, depending on the author, his audience, and the time of writing. It turns out that the story of the fig tree and the events associated with it clearly cannot be reconciled chronologically in both Gospels.

This serves as an illustration of the fact that New Testament books are based on real events, but they are theological in nature, not chronological.

Red Text in the Bible

The idea to highlight the words of Jesus in red was born at the very end of the nineteenth century, with the first version printed in 1901. However, commentators could not agree on the text of John, 3:13-21 where it wasn't clear if the words of Jesus end in vv. 11, 15, or 21. In the original text, no punctuation or quotation marks were used, and thus it is sometimes impossible to recognize where direct speech ended and the author's words followed. Thus, it is impossible to know to whom the words in John 3:13 belong (to John or Jesus):

> [13] No one has ever gone into heaven except the one who came from heaven, the Son of Man.

Most likely, this verse belongs to John. It reflects the birth of Jesus and His ascension into heaven. This may happen with the prophets when they themselves are not always able to understand whether the words belong to them or to God. It is quite possible that in the verses of John 3:13-21 the words of John and the words of Jesus are merged, where perhaps John himself could not distinguish where he ends and where Jesus starts teaching.

Context of the Old Testament Quotations

Context often drives the meaning of a verse. The context of the Old Testament verses mentioned by Peter in his letters carries more weight in their understanding. In Biblical times, the Old Testament was memorized by heart. The Jewish recipients of Peter's letters had no difficulty in grasping the context of these passages and would have shared their understanding with Gentile believers.

See, for example, 1 Peter 1:15-16:

> [15]...be holy in all you do; [16] for it is written: "Be holy, because I am holy."

At the first glance, it seems clear: the life of a believer must be righteous, and with that purpose Peter quotes Leviticus.

The following examples will illustrate the importance of the Old Testament context of Lev. 11:44-47:

> [44] I am the Lord your God; consecrate yourselves and be holy, because I am holy. And do not make yourselves unclean by any creature that moves about on the ground, [45] for I am the Lord who brought you up out the land of Egypt to be your God; and be holy, because I am holy. [46] This is the law regarding animals, birds, every living thing that moves in the water and every creature that moves about on the ground. [47] You must distinguish between the unclean and the clean, and between living creatures that may be eaten and those that may not be eaten.

The text in Leviticus speaks of observing the Law in relation to kosher food. But the text in Lev. 11:45, in turn, contains a quotation of the First commandment from Ex. 20:2:

> [2] I am the Lord your God, who brought you out of the land of Egypt, out of the house of slavery.

Another context leads to Lev. 19:2-4:

> [2] Speak to the entire assembly of Israel and say to them: Be holy because I, the Lord your God, am holy. [3] Each of you must respect

his mother and father, and you must observe my Sabbaths. I am the Lord your God. [4] Do not turn to idols and do not make gods of cast metal for yourselves. I am the Lord your God.

The first, second, fourth, and fifth commandments of the Law are mentioned here.

More context is found in Lev. 20:7-9, 26:

> [7] And consecrate yourselves and be holy, because I am the Lord your God. [8] And keep my decrees and follow them. I am the Lord, who makes you holy. [9] Anyone who curses his father or mother must be put to death. He has cursed his father or his mother, and his blood will be on his own head.
> [26] You are to be holy to me because I, the Lord, am holy...

The first and the fifth of the Ten Commandments are mentioned.

When all three contexts are analyzed on a broader level, our understanding of the New Testament's text expands.

In view of the context of the Old Testament, righteous behavior is consistent with the observance of the Law of Moses and is based on the First Commandment.

It may not coincide with behavioral norms in a society and could even contradict them.

In this example, the analysis of the context challenges the Church to exist in isolation from the Mosaic Law.

The quotations' context often leads to unexpected discoveries. The passages of the Bible gradually reveal their depth, and sometimes the precious "diamond" will be found, bringing the greatest joy. A solid theological basis is needed to achieve this goal, and the proper context for this is the entirety of the Scriptures from Genesis 1 up to Revelation 22.

Language Differences in the New Testament

Those who read the New Testament in translation know that all New Testament books are written in the same language, and in the same style, but it is the *translator's* style. This style changes from translation to translation, but it remains uniformly the same through all books of the same version.

While reading the New Testament in Greek, one will face the discovery that the language of the Gospel of Matthew and Paul's letters differs from the language in the Book of Revelation. Every author of the New Testament leaves a bit of himself in his book. The English translators of the King James Bible in 1611 believed that a special form of the Greek language was invented to write the divine New Testament. The science of linguistics denies even a slight possibility of such an endeavor. Later, at the end of the nineteenth century, theologians thought that the common people's language, *koine*, was the Greek of the New Testament. However, historians could not find the slightest trace of this *koine* in numerous first-century texts.

A new approach to this problem was discovered by chance. Twenty years later after the state of Israel was established, some missionaries decided to translate Luke's Gospel into Hebrew. The verses which were written in poor *koine* Greek surprisingly translated very easily into Hebrew, at which point the study of the Hebrew background of the New Testament started to be developed. Today, the influence of Hebrew on the Greek language of the New Testament is undeniable. Scientists only argue about what had slightly more influence on Greek of the New Testament: the Septuagint, or the fact that Jesus' disciples came from Galilee, where a mixture of Hebrew, Greek, and Aramaic languages was in use. Quotations from the Old Testament in the New Testament are roughly evenly divided between the Septuagint and the original Hebrew Bible.

Personal Names

In Biblical Hebrew, personal names often speak of the person's destiny or calling. For example, Moshe is the Hebrew name of Moses. While translating to Greek the sound "sh" was changed to "s," as there is no "sh" in Greek. The name received the masculine ending "s," which is a grammatical necessity of the Greek language. The name Moshe stands for "drawn out of the waters," which points to Ex. 2:5-10, but much more to Ex. 14:26-31, the crossing of the Red Sea.

Soon after the first Council of Nicaea, with the Church's departure from its Hebraic roots, personal names transliterated into Greek became part of the transition into Christian Scripture. Jewish names in the Bible were "lost in translation."

The Greek name Ἰησοῦς for Jesus is pronounced "Yay-soos." The Jewish name for Jesus is Yeshua, which has the meaning of "God saves" or "salvation."

The name of the mother of Jesus, in Greek Marias, was used in Matthew's Gospel for the first time (Matt. 1:16). Luke writes her name as Μαριάμ, Maryam, and her Hebrew name is "Miryam" (Luke 1:27). We find that Miryam was the name of Moses and Aaron's older sister (Ex. 15:20). The name's etymology is unclear.

The Greek names for anglicized Zechariah, Elizabeth, and John are Zakarias (Ζαχαρίας), Elisavet (Ἐλισάβετ), and Ioanes (Ἰωάννης). Their Hebrew meaning for Zekharya is "God remembers," Elisheva stands for "God has sworn, or God satisfies."[51] The Greek Ioanes is rooted in Hebrew Yokhanan, meaning "the LORD is gracious."

The name of Paul in Hebrew is "Shaul," "asked of God," while in Greek it is "Saulos." One modified letter and it turned out to be a Greek "Paulos," which means "small."

The four letters of the name יְהֹוָה, transliterated as YHWH, in many denominations is pronounced as "Jehovah" or "Yahweh," which probably should be read as the three-consonant word "Yehowah,"[52] with emphasis on the last syllable.

In Matt. 27:20-22 we read about "Barabbas" or more precisely in Hebrew BarAvva, which means "son of the Father." Sometimes Jesus called Himself "son of man," BarAdam. So, the crowd chose to release

---

51 One more meaning: God gave the seventh daughter.

52 Based on Masoretic codices and phonetic spelling of Strong number 3068.

the "son of the Father" but demanded the death of the "son of man" who was the true son of the Father and the God incarnate.

The pronunciations of these names as transmitted from teacher to student in the Masoretic tradition[53] from the rules applied in the Septuagint. In the Masoretic tradition, pronunciation rules were modified and became more complex over four centuries. This implies the existence of an oral tradition, where pronunciation rules can be verified. When one compares this to the simplified pronunciation rules in the Septuagint, clearly the Masoretic pronunciation is preferable.

Symbolic Numbers

Many of the New Testament books include numbers which are essential for the explanation of the content and messages or to justify the author's reasonings. Matthew and John do this frequently, using seven as the number for God, twelve as the number for Israel, and ten as any large number.

When taking numbers into account, we can identify seven parts in the Gospel of Matthew, which confirms that God is central in it. Similar to a textbook, the content is divided into logical parts. In John's Gospel, the student of the Bible reads about ten miracles and contemplates on ten parables. As ten is a symbol for a large number, this indicates that John has witnessed many more of them.

The genealogy of Jesus presented by Matthew adds up to fourteen descendants (Matt. 1:17). Biblically, His genealogy contains more ancestors, but Matthew intentionally used the number fourteen (or 7x2).

Gematria is the immensely popular system for calculating the numerical equivalence of letters, words, and, sometimes, phrases in the Hebrew text. The name "David" written in Hebrew has the numerical value of fourteen. The genealogy in Matt. 1:1-17 states three times that

---

53 Masoretic text - traditional codified Hebrew text of the Old Testament supplied with diacritical marks to enable correct pronunciation. This work was begun in the 6th century A.D. and completed in the 10th.

Jesus is the descendant of David, in other words, the Messiah. Obviously, Matthew was reasoning in Hebrew.

While Jesus reminded his disciples of the number of bread loaves combining five and seven, totaling twelve, this brought them to the conclusion that it was not about bread, but about all of Israel (Matt. 16:9-11). In Matt. 23:13-29, we read that Jesus speaks the words "Woe to you" seven times, making it clear that this is the judgment of God. In Matt. 4:2 Jesus fasted for forty days and forty nights, which is clearly related to the forty years of Israel's wanderings in the wilderness (Num. 14:34):

> [34] You will bear the consequences of your iniquities forty years based on the number of the forty days that you scouted the land, a year for each day.

Although the numerical symbolism only complements the author's idea, it should be a companion in interpretation. After all, it often confirms the author's intention.

See Rev. 13:11, 16-18:

> [11] And I saw another beast, coming out of the earth. He had two horns like a lamb, and he spoke like a dragon...
> [16] And he also forced everyone, and small, and great, and rich, and poor, and free, and slave, to receive a mark on his right hand or on his forehead, [17] and that no one could buy or sell unless he had the mark, which is the name of the beast or the number of his name. [18] This calls for wisdom. If anyone has understanding, let him calculate the number of the beast, and it is man's number, and his number is 666.

The image of the beast with two horns as an idol comes from Ex. 32:1-20. John connects the cult of the emperor with idolatry, reminding the reader that Moses has smashed the idol into dust. The order of the beast brings a different analogy from Deut. 6:8, 11:18 and Ex. 13:16. Through the ages, observant Jewish males wear *tefillin* or phylacteries during the weekday morning prayers to fulfill the Torah's instructions to keep them as a "sign." The arm-*tefillah* should be placed on the upper left arm, while the head-*tefillah* is placed on the forehead.

The *tefillin's* boxes contain the handwritten parchments with Biblical verses with either the Shema Israel prayer (Deut. 6:4-9), or the commandment to keep the commandments (Deut. 11:13-21), or to remember of the Exodus (Ex. 13:1-10), or to educate children (Ex. 13:11-16).

Satan replaces the words of God with his own sign: he forces the sign on the right arm, as opposed to the left arm, to display who this person really worships.

The deification of the Roman emperor by the population of the Empire was confirmed by the collection of a small tax. Without this tax receipt, one was considered the enemy of the Empire and was treated accordingly. Christians often requested that their neighbors pay tax on their behalf to evade this unpopular rule.

In the Middle East, the letters had numerical value, so it was possible to calculate the meaning of each name. All speculations based on the interpretation of the number 666 do not take into account that the Arabic numbers came into use a thousand years after the first century.

However, the number 666 reflects John's Jewish reasoning. This number is the gematria on the name of the Roman emperor Nero, written in Greek and translated into Hebrew, where the Hebrew letters are replaced by numbers. The second variant 616 is found in some copies. Its gematria stands for the name of Nero in Latin, translated into Hebrew.

Since the Jews, like all Semitic peoples, loved analogy, and Nero and Domitian both persecuted Christians, it was possible to substitute the name of one emperor with another following *gezera shava*. Consequently, both emperors lost the battle with God. The Revelation prophecy was fulfilled a year later when Domitian was killed by his own Praetorian guard.

Knowledge of Historical Context

With a knowledge of the Biblical historical context, the "why, when, and where" details of any given passage make it come alive and reveal its importance to the original audience.

For example, see Matt. 8:5-13:

> [5] And when Jesus had entered Capernaum [Kfer Nahum], a centurion came to him, asking for help, [6] and saying, "Lord, my servant lies at home without a movement and in terrible suffering." [7] And Jesus said to him, "I will go and heal him." [8] And the centurion replied, saying, "Lord, I do not deserve to have you come under my roof. But just say the word, and my servant will be healed. [9] And I myself a man under authority, with soldiers under me. And I tell one, 'Go,' and he goes; and another, 'Come,' and he comes. And I say to my servant, 'Do this,' and he does it." [10] And when Jesus heard this, he was astonished and said to those following him, "I tell you the truth, I have not found even in Israel such great faith. [11] And I say to you that many will come from the east and the west, and will recline with Abraham, and Isaac, and Jacob in the kingdom of heaven. [12] And the subjects of the kingdom will be thrown outside, into the darkness, where there will be weeping and gnashing of teeth." [13] And Jesus said to the centurion, "Go, it will be done just as you believed it would." And his servant was healed at that very hour.

The centurion arriving with a request for his servant's healing was not an ordinary event.

In Judea, especially in Galilee, there were no Roman legions.[54] The governor of Judea had the rank of a prefect (military title) and commanded five cohorts of 480 men each, and a cavalry squadron of sixty soldiers. One of these cohorts, the Cohors I Sebastenorum, was stationed in Jerusalem, with the rest of the troops being stationed in Caesarea Maritima. During the feast of Pesach (Passover) the population of Jerusalem swelled to five times the usual quantity. It was necessary for the Roman prefect Pontius Pilate,[55] along with an additional cohort, to arrive each year at Jerusalem. These two cohorts, which were at the disposal of the Roman governor, were the strongest part of the half

---

54 Cohors Prima Augusta, Cohors Prima Italica Civium Romanorum, Cohors Secunda Italica Civium Romanorum, Cohors I Sebastenorum and the cavalry band Ala I Sebastenorum. "The Roman Army in Judaea under the Procurators", in M.P. Speidel, Roman Army Studies II, (1992) Stuttgart. pp. 224-232.

55 The civil title of procurator was given to Pontius Pilate for his successful service in Judea.

legion. The irregular auxiliary forces, Cohors Tumultuaria, were the Roman equivalent of a police force, inferior in terms of combat readiness, were present everywhere and were led by Roman centurions. This centurion was responsible for maintaining order throughout Galilee and he was the chief of police in the small kingdom of Herod the Great's son in Galilee. In the modern army, the rank of centurion corresponds to the ranks from captain to colonel. The centurion probably had a junior rank.

The rank of centurion could be achieved by a Roman legionnaire holding the position of the centurion's first deputy, with three recommendations by the higher commanders. The candidate should be at least thirty years old. By that time, the candidate for the position of centurion would spend fifteen years in the army and had to prove that he had the character of a commander.

Sudden inspections of remote posts, conversations with the local people, and double accountability to the local king and the Roman prefect indicate that this centurion had to be a practical and determined man who knew how to get along with everyone and stand up for his own.

In many commentaries Capernaum is described as a city with a population of 15,000 to 25,000[56] with a Roman garrison of soldiers stationed there. As suggested in the commentaries, the centurion had to deal with the large toll collection service for passage through the city.

It is very unlikely that this centurion lived in Capernaum. The settlement at the time of Jesus was very small, never had a fortification wall, and was located between the shore of the lake and the cemetery outside it.[57] The size of the settlement at its heyday covered roughly fifteen acres. This means that the number of people living there in the first century was between 350 and 400,[58] including children. In the time of

---

56 Jonathan L. Reed, Archaeology and the Galilean Jesus: a re-examination of the evidence (2002) 149.

57 Travelers in the 4th century, at the heyday of the Capernaum, described it as a small village. Jonathan L. Reed, Archaeology and the Galilean Jesus: a re-examination of the evidence (2002) 141.

58 Hayim Lapin, Economy, geography, and provincial history in later Roman Palestine (2001) 118.

Jesus, the settlement was estimated to be roughly 600 by 900 feet, with three or four streets.[59] The towns Gush Halav and Meyron were almost 1.5 times larger than Capernaum, and their population was reported to be about 500 people.[60] In addition, the size of the towns was confirmed by the presence and the size of their synagogues. On Saturday, Capernaum's synagogue was supposed to accommodate the entire town population and was built for about 400 people. All synagogues served as centers of public life and schools for children's education and were never empty.

There was no bustling traffic through Capernaum, nor was it difficult to get around it. Since there was no towered wall or river with a drawbridge, taxes were not collected from travelers. But the local fishing industry was reasonably taxed. One had to pay the tax on every catch, every fish,[61] and thus the tax collector had his place on the shore of the Sea of Galilee. In addition, it was essential to have proper skills to collect the taxes from fishermen.

According to archaeological evidence, there was a Roman mile post in such an insignificant place as Capernaum from the beginning of the second century, which proves the extensive civil order of the Roman Empire.

There was no job for a chief of police in a place like Capernaum. For comparison, about 120 people might have lived in eighteen houses in Nazareth. Most likely, the centurion lived in Tiberias, the capital of Galilee, a city founded by Herod Antipas in 19 A.D. on the former site of the village of Reket, nine miles south of Capernaum, which became the capital of the kingdom in 26 A.D. The city itself was about a half square mile, with a population of about 30,000. The size of the kingdom suggests that more than twenty soldiers were stationed in Tiberias, and the rest were placed in small posts in the rest of the kingdom.

---

59 Richard A. Horsley, Galilee: history, politics, people (1995) 194.

60 ibid., 194.

61 K. C. Hanson, The Galilean Fishing Economy and the Jesus Tradition Biblical Theology Bulletin 27 (1997) 99-111.

This centurion did not build the synagogue in Capernaum. Archaeological analysis of Capernaum's only synagogue date it to the fifth century, at the peak of Capernaum's prosperity. The synagogue of the time of Jesus was not found,[62] probably because of its insignificant size, as well as reconstructions and expansions in later years.

Most likely, the centurion built a new synagogue in Tiberias about a year before he met Jesus in Capernaum, as written in Luke 7:5:

> [5] because he loves our people and has built our synagogue.

Thus, the centurion's arrival in Capernaum was deliberate, as a result of the reports received by him from his subordinates. It was reasonable for him to establish surveillance on Jesus and His followers. The crowd of Jesus' followers, thousands of people, naturally could not be left "unsupervised." Galilee was also the place of many uprisings and riots, historically, and thus at least three observers should have been present.

This centurion was aware of all the events and miracles of Jesus and His disciples. When he received the message that Jesus was going to Capernaum, he decided to ask about the healing of his servant and rode his horse to Capernaum; all centurions in the Roman army had horses. Of course, the police observers also sent their reports with the riders, because the situation could change very quickly. And it was not difficult to find Jesus with a large crowd in a few streets of Capernaum.

Considering the historical context, the passage should be presented as the story of the encounter and interaction of Jesus and the centurion. The police chief and Roman officer had to oversee the activities of Jesus and his disciples. The man was knowledgeable, intelligent, and determined. It is critical to understand that this man, the first Gentile believer, accepted Jesus as his Messiah and the Messiah of Israel. He worships Jesus in heaven along with Abraham, and Isaac, and Jacob.

---

62 The foundation, which has survived to our time, cannot be confidently identified with the synagogue of the first century.

Knowledge of Judaism

Knowledge of Judaism was never a requirement for Christians. More-over, for the most part, it was not encouraged throughout the history of Christianity. Meanwhile, this knowledge (or the lack of it) is vital and critical for Christian life.

In the history of Judaism, the rabbinical version of the Ten Command-ments of the Mosaic Law was taught as valid for Gentile believers. The list of these commandments kept changing over time. Faithful obser-vance of these commandments by Gentile believers and their faith in the Jewish Messiah guarantee their place in the Kingdom of Heaven as well as being *righteous according to the Law of Moses* on an equal footing with Jewish believers. Gentile believers are called *ger toshav* in Hebrew, aliens among Israel, or righteous Gentiles. That is how Abraham named himself in Gen. 23:4, גֵּר וְתוֹשָׁב. The NIV translation as "alien and a stranger" does not communicate these nuances.

According to Rabbinical Judaism the following commandments are not difficult to observe:

Believe in God — Ex. 20:2
Not to have other gods — Ex. 20:5
Not to commit premeditated murder — Ex. 20:13
Do not steal — Ex. 20:15
Do not commit adultery — Ex. 20:14
Do not blaspheme — Ex. 22:28

Judaism views anti-Semitism as idolatry. While being enslaved in Egypt the Jews had neither an army nor their own land. Nevertheless, they faced the first anti-Semitic attack described in the Bible. The Pha-raoh set his mind on destroying all Jewish people. The Bible describes the events as the confrontation of Egyptian gods and the Hebrew God.

In the New Testament there is no *direct* indication of the righteousness of Gentile believers in accordance with the Law's commandments but only *indirect* ones. Out of all authors of the New Testament, only Mat-thew and Mark remained silent on this subject, as they did not address the character of the Church. Paul wrote the important letter to the

Church with *only* Gentile believers (Phil. 1:1):

> ¹ Paul and Timothy, servants of Christ Jesus, to all the saints in Christ Jesus at Philippi, together with the overseers and deacons.

Since the saints, by definition, are righteous and justified, Gentile Christians are *already* righteous, and therefore the process of sanctification and justification is *not needed*. The only passage in the New Testament where Gentile believers are *not* called righteous is in Gal. 3:1:

> ¹ O *blockhead* Galatians! Who has *swindled* you? It was before your eyes that Jesus Christ was publicly portrayed as crucified.

Paul accused Gentile believers in the Galatian Church of seeking additional righteousness to obtain, as they considered righteousness according to the Law as insufficient. The moment they perceived themselves as *unjust*, they became unjust. That is why Paul addressed them so differently.

Gentile believers are not under the curse of the Law for not keeping it, and their behavioral boundaries are fully consistent with the words of Jesus in Matt. 11:30: "my yoke is easy."

Overall believers are declared either justified, or saints, or righteous in 120 different verses in the New Testament. The existence of valid commandments for Gentile Christians changes concepts of adoption, justification, and sanctification most significantly, but the full scope of this important theme goes beyond the purpose of this book. It is only necessary to emphasize that justification of a believer in the Old and New Testament is initiated by God.

Knowledge of the Bible

Building up a deep knowledge of the Bible is a great challenge, but such knowledge leads to a greater closeness to God and helps us to grow in our faith in Him.

The following commentary on Rev. 2:12-17 can serve as an illustration of the sufficiency and dynamic nature of the Scriptures:

[12] To the angel [*secretary*] of the church in Pergamum write: These are the words of him who has the sharp, double-edged sword. [13] I know where you live, where Satan has his throne. Yet you remain true to my name. You did not renounce my faith, even in the days of my faithful witness Antipas, who was put to death in your city where Satan lives. [14] Nevertheless, I have a few things against you: You have people there who hold to the teaching of Balaam, who taught Balak to put a stumbling block before the sons of Israel by eating food sacrificed to idols and by committing sexual immorality. [15] And you also have those who hold to the teaching of the Nicolaitans. [16] And repent, and if not I will come to you soon and will fight against them with the sword of my mouth. [17] He who has an ear, let him hear what the Spirit says to the churches. To him who overcomes, I will give some of the hidden manna. And I will give him a white stone with a new name written on it, which no one knows but he who receives it.

Throughout Church history multiple theories attempted to find the explanation for the kind of angels in Rev. 2 and 3 to whom the Apostle John allegedly wrote the messages. Those theories explained the place angels live, what their names are, what churches they inhabit or not, how to see those angels, and why John should write letters to them. The original readers of the Book of Revelation, as well as Jews nowadays, would refer to the elected messenger and elder in any synagogue as *Shaliach Tzibbur* in Hebrew. Being a worship leader, he reads out the correspondence addressed to the entire congregation. Since "messenger" and "angel" carry the same connotation, the description could be easily misunderstood. The word *Shaliach* comes from the Hebrew verb *shalach* which means "to send" (as a messenger), and *Tzibbur* stands for "congregation" or "community" in Hebrew.

The name Balaam or *Bilam* literally means "not of the people," i.e., Gentile (Num. 22-25, 31:15-16). He could not directly pronounce curses on the Jews, but he advised King Balak, whose name literally means "destroyer," how to push the Israelis away from God.

John's reasoning in Rev. 2:14 could also be interpreted in this way: those who adhered to that doctrine of the pagans led by Satan, who taught the Destroyer to lead Jews away from God.

He who has an ear, let him hear: this phrase is taken from Ezek. 12:2, but it is better to read it within the context of Ezek. 12:1-6. The quotation is far from flattering and shows that the hearers of the Book of Revelation are a sign to unbelieving Jews. The faith of Gentile believers would be the "sign for the house of Israel." John repeats this quotation in all letters to all Churches to call them to fulfill their purpose. Here John follows the footsteps of Apostle Paul (Rom. 11:11).

What about the promise of the hidden manna? The word "manna" comes from the Hebrew word *man* and relates to the Hebrew phrase "what is it?" See Ex. 16:13-15:

> [15] When the Israelites saw it, they asked one another, "What is it?" because they didn't know what it was.

Manna is also called "the bread of angels" in Ps. 78:24-25. The verse contains the straightforward reference to Deut. 8:3. Manna comes only from God.

The research on the white stone in Rev. 2:17 leads us to the Old Testament. The Lord commanded the creation of sacred garments for Aaron serving as the high priest. The breastplate was decorated with twelve precious stones representing each tribe of Israel (Ex. 28:15-29). The stone in the first row, *Yahalom* in Hebrew, carries the tribe's name Zebulun or Zevulun. Matt. 4 connects us to Isa. 9.

See Matt. 4:13-14:

> [13] And leaving Nazareth, he went and lived in Capernaum, which was by the sea in the territory of Zebulun and Naphtali [14] to fulfill what was said through the prophet Isaiah...

Isa. 9:1-2:

> [1] But there will be no *more* gloom for her who was in anguish; in earlier times He treated the land of Zebulun and the land of Naphtali with contempt, but later on He shall make *it* glorious, by the way of the sea, on the other side of Jordan, Galilee of the Gentiles. [2] The people who walk in darkness will see a great light; those who live in a dark land, the light will shine on them.

Nazareth being the original home and Capernaum as the base of Jesus' ministry take place within the borders of the land assigned to the descendants of Zebulun and Naftali.

The new name written on white[63] stone belongs to Jesus, and those who receive it are His followers.

Synoptic Gospels

As noted above, the four Gospels were originally composed in a different chronological order than their ordering in the New Testament. The formation of the canonical Gospels (Matthew, Mark, and Luke) would be properly understood by placing them in a first-century Jewish context, before the destruction of the Temple. The word "synoptic" comes from the Greek *synoptikos*, meaning "able to be seen together."

Roughly 90% of Mark's Gospel is reflected in Matthew's Gospel, and roughly 53% of it is found in Luke's Gospel. If Matthew was indeed the first evangelist, there would be no need for Mark to write a separate book. If Mark's Gospel were written first, then Matthew and Luke complemented it in their writings.

Why was Matthew's Gospel placed first in the New Testament? According to Replacement Theology, the Church, "free" of Jewish influence, replaced Israel. Since Matthew's Gospel was addressed to a *Jewish* audience, and Mark's Gospel to a *Gentile* audience, Matthew's was intentionally placed at the beginning. Thus, Mark's Gospel "complements" and "improves" it. In fact, Matthew's Gospel is the most challenging book to understand in the New Testament. Luke's Gospel is erroneously considered the most "Gentile" book, as a text that serves to show the progression from Jewish to Gentile believers.

Many verses in the Gospels of Matthew and Luke coincide, which suggests the existence of the additional text that has served as a basis. Matthew, Luke, and Mark drew on a common oral tradition followed by the early Church, which explains the patterns of differences and similarities. The written documents were not discovered.

---

63 According to the Jewish tradition *yahalom* was white.

Elements of Replacement Theology, and most Christian denominations' commitment to them, contradict the Scriptures in many ways.

Erroneous Translation

From time to time we may find some innocent and harmless mistakes in translations of the New Testament. However, sometimes they result in erroneous teachings.

Without the Law

As noted above, the Greek word *anomos*, "without the Law" or "without the Law of Moses" is found in twenty-nine verses in the New Testament. *Anomos* is a regular word, built according to the rules of the Greek language, as the negation of the word "law," *nomos*.[64] The word *anomos* and its variants have been translated into English as "lawlessness," "lawless deeds," "transgression," "iniquity," "unrighteousness," "wicked," etc., which is misleading. When translated correctly in accordance with the original text, the Church teaching would be in constant conflict with the Scriptures.

Other distortions of the New Testament's text call for our attention. For example, most translations use the word "unlawful" or "forbidden" as in Acts 10:28, where the original text does not have the word "Law":

> [28] And he said to them: "You are well aware that it is *not acceptable* for a Jew to associate with a Gentile or visit him. But God has shown me that I should not call any man impure or unclean.

Incorrect translation gives the impression that Mosaic Law prohibits Jews to associate with Gentiles. In reality, it was stipulated by the rabbinic tradition.

Many commentators state that Jesus abrogated the Mosaic Law on clean and unclean food given in Lev. 11 and Deut. 14 by the statement in Mark 7:19 (NIV):

> [19]...In saying this, Jesus declared all foods "clean."

---

64 Jean Bottéro, Clarisse Herrenschmidt, Jean Pierre Vernant, Ancestor of the West (2000) 97.

Even Jewish New Testament version followed this reasoning. The statement misreads, mistranslates, and misquotes Bible in Greek, which states in Mark 7:14-19:

> [14] Summoning the crowd again, he told them, "Listen to me, all of you, and understand: [15] Nothing that goes into a person from outside can defile him but the things that come out of a person are what defile him."...
>
> [17] When he went into the house away from the crowd, his disciples asked him about the *parable*. [18] He said to them, "Are you also as lacking in understanding? Don't you realize that nothing going into a person from the outside can defile him? [19] For it doesn't go into his heart but into the stomach and *goes out into the latrine*" (*cleansing all the foods* [from the body]).

The sentence in parentheses is not found in many manuscripts. Building theology on such a deceptive basis should be avoided.

The word "cleansing," καθαρίζων, is a dangling participle, which sometimes occurs in translations from Hebrew to Greek and leads to confusion. In this case, the masculine verb "cleanse" points to the previous masculine noun "latrine."

The definite article τὰ limits foods to that which is already in the body. Consequently, many translations, which state that Jesus declared all foods "clean," make a false statement.

Jesus is presenting a parable on the sin of unbelief and disobedience to God which defiles a man (Mark 7:14-23). Eating the unclean food in Israel was an act of disobedience. Unfortunately, the *deliberate* mistranslation of any Biblical text must be defined as an act of disobedience.

It is not uncommon to hear people say that the Letter to the Hebrews teaches that the Mosaic commandments are weak and useless, and that Jesus annulled the law of Moses (Heb. 7:18-19):

> [18] The former regulation is set aside because it was weak and useless [19] (for the law made nothing perfect).

The expression "former regulation," προαγούσης ἐντολῆς, as "previous commandment" is in singular form. That previous commandment as found in Heb. 7:16 describes the replacement of the High Priest's post by Jesus.

The word "set aside" transliterated in Greek as *athetésis*, literally means "no longer having a place." With the imminent destruction of the Temple, all commandments which regulated the sacrificial system would become moot.

The words "weak and useless" in Greek should be translated as "not strong and not beneficial" when applied to the Law in the absence of the Temple services.

The word "perfect," ἐτελείωσεν, refers to a state of accomplishment. Thus, the text in Heb. 7:20 continues an explanation showing that these verses are not about annulment of the Law, but are rather about changes in the priesthood with the loss of the Temple.

Thus Heb. 7:18-19 should be translated the following way:

> [18] The previous commandment is no longer having the place because it was not strong and not beneficial [19] and the [Temple] Law accomplished nothing. and a better hope is introduced, by which we draw near to God.

Gentiles

The crux of the matter is a mistranslation of the word "nations" that affects the interpretation of the Great Commission (Matt. 28:19):

> [19] And go and make disciples of all *nations*, baptizing them in the name of the Father and of the Son and of the Holy Spirit."

The proper translation should be:

> [19] And go and make disciples of all *Gentiles*, baptizing them in the name of the Father and of the Son and of the Holy Spirit."

The Greek word ἔθνη used in Matthew can be found in 148 verses of the New Testament. It is translated into English by five different words: nations, pagans, people, heathen, Gentiles. In addition, the word "Greeks" with the same meaning occurs in twenty verses.

The translation reflects the fact that New Testament authors reasoned in Hebrew, and thus they intended the word *goyim* (plural) to stand for "not Jews", Gentiles. When referring to Israel, the meaning can be negative, i.e., Ezek. 2:3:

> ³ And He said to me, "Son of man, I am sending you to the sons of Israel, to the rebellious *Gentiles* [goyim] who have rebelled against Me.

Here, *goyim* has the meaning of "those who do not believe in God." The Septuagint translates *goyim* as *ethne* 703 times. One of these verses is Isa. 11:10:

> ¹⁰ And in that day there shall be a root of Jesse, which shall stand for an ensign of the people; to it shall the *Gentiles* seek: and his rest shall be glorious.

In the New Testament, perhaps, *ethne* means "Gentile nations" only in Acts 13:19. Everywhere else it should be translated as Gentiles.

The translation of *goyim* as *ethne* can be seen in Acts 13:47:

> ⁴⁷ And thus the Lord has commanded us [Paul and Barnabas]: I have made you [singular] a light for the Gentiles, and you [singular, Messiah] will be for salvation to the ends of the earth.

The quotation brings us to Isa. 42:6, 49:6 (LXX), where the Hebrew word *goyim* is *correctly* represented by the Greek *ethne*. In some English translations there is an attempt to replace the statement (on the Messiah being the light for the Gentiles in order to save them) with the claim that the Church would bring salvation. In translation the word "you" (Acts 13:47), by applying plural instead of singular, refers to the Church which allegedly replaced Israel. Here Paul and Barnabas make the messianic statement based on Isa. 42:6 (NIV):

> ⁶...I will keep you [singular] and will make you [Messiah] to be a covenant for the people [singular, Israel] and a light for the Gentiles,

The following is the translations of Mark 7:26 found in NIV/KJV:

> 26 And the woman was a Greek, a Syrophoenician by birth. She begged Jesus to drive the demon out of her daughter.

Since the Phoenicians had nothing to do with the Greeks, it would be more appropriate to translate it more in alignment with Mark's intention:

> 26 And the woman was a *Gentile*, a Syrophoenician by birth. She begged Jesus to drive the demon out of her daughter.

Greeks were part of the Gentile world to the Jews.

Compare with the verse in Acts 18:4:

> 4 And every Sabbath he reasoned in the synagogue, trying to persuade Jews and *Greeks*."

Even though Corinth was in Greece, its Gentile population consisted not only of Greeks. The correct translation can be found only in the CEV version:

> 4 And every Sabbath he reasoned in the synagogue, trying to persuade Jews and *Gentiles*.

The same approach brings more weight to Matt. 28:19. Jesus gave the new commission to His disciples. It is important to note that He sent His disciples only to the Jews initially (Matt. 10:5-7):

> 5 These twelve Jesus sent out with the following instructions: "Do not go among the Gentiles or enter any town of the Samaritans. 6Go rather to the lost sheep of Israel. 7As you go, preach this message: 'The kingdom of heaven is near.'"

From now on they had to bring the Gospel message to all other people, which implies that Jewish evangelism is mandated by the Messiah. The Church should *always* carry the Gospel to the Jews. This "great omission" to the Great Commission regarding Jewish evangelism is gradually being remedied. However, over the period of two millennia, numerous explanations have been developed to justify dodging this command.

Synagogue

The original text of James 2:2 reads as follows:

> [2] And if a man comes into your *synagogue* wearing gold ring and sparklingly white clothes, and comes a poor man in old shabby clothes.

Compare it with the NIV translation:

> [2] Suppose a man comes into your meeting wearing a gold ring and fine clothes, and a poor man in shabby clothes also comes in.

Investigating the text, we find the interpreters' bias in most versions. Their reasoning is straightforward. Gentile Christians do not go to a synagogue, and Jews do not go to a church.

The word here in Greek, and everywhere else in the New Testament, is synagogue, not an assembly or a meeting. The Jewish believers of Jesus, along with Gentile believers, met in synagogues on every Sabbath, where several scrolls of Scriptures were housed to be read and studied.

Meanwhile, both words and their application were well known to James (James 5:14):

> [14] Is anyone among you sick? He should call for the elders of the *ecclesia*, and they are to pray over him, anointing him with oil in the name of the Lord.

The Greek word συναγωγή, synagogue, can be found fifty-seven times in the New Testament and 195 times in the Septuagint. It may be translated as "assembly" *if* it is not related to Israel, as in Ezek. 38:15:

> [13] Sheba and Dedan and the merchants of Tarshish with all its rulers will ask you, "Have you come to seize spoil? Have you mobilized your *assembly* to carry off plunder...

When the word συναγωγή refers to Israel, then it should always be translated as synagogue.

Church

A similar mistranslation took place with the word "church" in some versions of the Bible, See Acts 7:38:

> [38] He was in the *church* [ecclesia] in the desert, with the angel who spoke to him on Mount Sinai, and with our fathers; and he received living words to pass on to us.

The Greek word *ecclesia* is translated here as an "assembly" by CSB, NAS, NAB, as "congregation" in NASB, and in all other instances as "church." It seems that this conclusion comes from the interpretation of the event from the time of Moses, but the Church has nothing to do with the Law and with the Jews; rather, it was taught that the translation should fit the Church's theology.

The word *ecclesia* often occurs in the Septuagint in a strictly religious context to describe the Jews who believe in God, and this supports a *continuity* of the Church with Israel.

The Bible states that *ecclesia* was established by Moses; the first time that *ecclesia* is mentioned is in Lev. 8:3, and thus Luke follows the established tradition (Lev. 8:1-3, LXX):

> [8:1] The Lord said to Moses, [2] "Bring Aaron and his sons, their garments, the anointing oil, the bull for the sin offering, the two rams and the basket containing bread made without yeast, [3] and gather the entire assembly [ecclesia] at the entrance to the Tent of Meeting."

The Greek word *ecclesia*, as an exception, may be translated as "assembly" *if* it is not related to believers in God. One of three such occurrences is in Acts 19:32 describing the riot against Paul:

> [32] The assembly was in confusion: Some were shouting one thing, some another. Most of the people did not even know why they were there.

Aramaic Language

Sometimes translators claim that the Jews of the time of Jesus spoke Aramaic in eight verses: John 5:2, 19:13, 17, 20, 20:16, Acts 21:40, 22:2, 26:14.

For example, Acts 21:40:

> [40] Having received the commander's permission, Paul stood on the steps and motioned to the crowd. When they were all silent, he said to them in Aramaic.

The word in Greek Ἑβραΐδι means *Hebrew,* not "Aramaic."

We find the correct translation in Acts 6:1, Phil. 3:5, Rev. 9:11, 16:16, 2 Cor. 11:22, when the text makes any other translation impossible:

> [22] Are they *Hebrews* [Ἑβραῖοί]? So am I. Are they Israelites? So am I. Are they Abraham's descendants? So am I.

The word "Hebrew" comes from Gen. 14:13:

> [13] One who had escaped came and reported this to Abram the Hebrew [*Haibri*]. Now Abram was living near the great trees of Mamre the Amorite, a brother of Eshcol and Aner, all of whom were allied with Abram.

The reasoning is rooted in the idea that the Jews did not know Hebrew. Thus, they did not know how to read their own Scriptures, and the Church kept up the "correct" explanation. The fallacy of that idea is obvious given that we have a multitude of documents in Hebrew and the Masoretic Old Testament with preserved words' spellings, as well as parts of the Talmud written in Hebrew. None of the New Testament authors used the Targum (translation of the Old Testament in Aramaic), except for one instance in Paul's writings.

Heart

Many believe that the heart is the place of one's emotions. We can find Christian denominations where emotions and feelings are given great emphasis. Moreover, charismatic teachings that are quite simple, attractive, and popular, but not without some anti-intellectual tendencies, draw the greatest attention. One of the outcomes of this situation is a lack of Biblical knowledge, where there is no place for feelings in the heart. In Biblical times, feelings were believed to be in the stomach, or guts, and the head was the seat of a headache.

The word heart represents the most important and vital part in the description of a problem or a city or a human. In ancient times people did not have the science of anatomy; thus, the words *lev*, לֵב, and *levav*, לֵבָב, may stand for "heart" in Hebrew, but they also mean intellect or mind or reasoning. That is why the heart and mind cannot be in opposition to one another. According to James, we may find the solution for double-mindedness (James 4:8):

> [8] Draw near to God, and he will draw near to you. Cleanse your hands, sinners, and purify your hearts, you double-minded.

Translations in English do not convey the two different words used for the description of the heart (Isa. 6:10):

> [10] Make the heart [*lev*] of this people calloused, make their ear dull and close their eye. Otherwise, they might see with their eye, hear with their ear, understand with their heart [*levav*], and turn and be healed."

The word "repent" in Hebrew stands for turning back and moving in the right direction. Isaiah applied *lev* to poor intelligence, similar to that of a child, but *levav* is used in the case of higher intelligence, as in adults.

Biblical teaching on the heart can be found in Deut. 6:5-6:

> [5] And love the Lord your God with all your heart [*levav*] and with all your soul and with all your strength. [6] And these words that I command you today are to be in your heart [*levav*].

The word *levav* is the heart of the believer in God here.

God's Law can only be in the human mind (Deut. 30:14):

> [14] But the word is very near you; it is in your mouth and in your heart [*levav*] so you may obey it.

Ps. 14:1, 53:1:

> ¹ The fool says in his heart [*lev*], "There is no God."

There is blasphemy in his heart, and thus he is a fool with a childish small mind.

Here is a direct explanation (Prov. 22:15):

> ¹⁵ Folly is bound up in the heart [*lev*] of a child, but the rod of discipline will drive it far from him.

Feelings do not produce foolishness, but the activity of the mind.

While writing in Greek, Mark's reasoning brings up the Hebrew *lev* (Mark 7:21):

> ²¹ And from within, out of people's hearts, come evil thoughts, sexual immorality, theft, murder, adultery,

Paul argues that a believer in God belongs to Israel, Rom. 2:28-29:

> ²⁸ For a person is not a Jew who is one outwardly, and true circumcision is not something visible in the flesh. ²⁹ On the contrary, a person is a Jew who is one inwardly, and circumcision is of the *heart...*

The following verses address feelings, in Hebrew רֶחֶם, transliterated as *racham* and defined as inward parts, which are the place for different feelings (Gen. 43:30):

> ³⁰ And Joseph made haste; for his *inward parts* did yearn upon his brother: and he sought to weep; and he entered into chamber, and wept there.

In Greek σπλάγχνα is transliterated as *splanchna*, Phile. 7, 12, 20:

> ⁷ Your love has given me great joy and encouragement, because you, brother, have refreshed the *inward parts* of the saints...
> ¹² I am sending him, who is in my *inward parts* back to you...
> ²⁰ I do wish, brother, that I may have some benefit from you in the Lord; refresh my *inward parts* in Christ.

Paul speaks of guts in 2 Cor. 6:11:

> [12] We are not straitened in us, and you are straitened in your own *inward parts*.

He writes about Titus in 2 Cor. 7:15:

> [15] And his *inward parts* are more abundant toward you.

Exaggerated Language

It was a common practice for all Semitic people including Jews to use exaggerated sayings, hyperbole, metaphorical and idiomatic language, aphorisms, parables, and even sarcasm. The student of the Bible may discern the case of an exaggerated saying when it conflicts with what Jesus says in other Biblical verses, and/or with teachings of the Old Testament. Those who are not accustomed to this practice do not always recognize it.

See Matt. 3:7:

> [7] When he saw many of the Pharisees and Sadducees coming to his baptism, he said to them, "Brood of vipers! Who warned you to flee from the coming wrath?"

John does not make any exceptions when addressing the Pharisees and Sadducees. Nicodemus, one of the Pharisees' leaders, is the proof of the exception (John 3:1, 7:50, 19:39). The exaggeration is the use of the snake image, taken from Gen. 3:1, which is an insult for the leaders of religious people; in addition, snakes do not belong to the Pharisees' ancestors.

The words "all" and "no one" are not really all-encompassing or exclusive words, and are often outright exaggerations. There seems to be no exaggeration in the text of John 3:13:

> [13] And no one has ever gone up into heaven except the one who came from heaven: the Son of Man.

See the text of 2 Kings 2:11:

> [11] And it came to pass as they were walking along and talking together, and suddenly a chariot of fire and horses of fire appeared and separated the two of them, and went up Elijah by a whirlwind into heaven.

Elijah was undoubtedly taken up to heaven. Is the ascension to heaven in a chariot "taken into account," or should one come down from heaven first? In any case, there is a possibility of exaggeration here.

So far, the examples above do not affect the text's meaning. Let us examine cases where the exaggeration influences not only the meaning of the text, but also impacts our understanding of the New Testament and its theology.

Usually, these verses are used to prove that all men are sinners and that the Law of Moses contradicts the righteousness of God. Traditionally, these verses are not accepted as an exaggeration, (Rom. 3:10-12):

> [10] As it is written: "There is no one righteous, not even one; [11] there is no one who understands, no one who seeks God. [12] All have turned away, they all together have become worthless; there is no one who does good, not even one."

The following verse is considered a clear example of exaggeration, (Rom. 11:26):

> [26] And so all Israel will be saved, as it is written: "The deliverer will come from Zion; and he will turn godlessness away from Jacob.

There is a plethora of comments that "prove" that "all Israel" does not mean all Israelites, nor the majority, nor even the minority, but its insignificant remnant.

The verses in Rom. 3:10-12 lead us to Ps. 14:1, which teaches that all are guilty before God without exception, but the quotation is incomplete and altered by Paul. In David's Psalm the text begins: "The fool says in his heart, there is no God."

In these verses, David speaks of an unbeliever (the fool) who seeks to justify his unbelief in God. The word "all" is intended to describe only the unbelievers. Anyone who knows the Old Testament can find the exaggeration in Paul's argument. It is amazing how sarcastic the Bible can be about those unbelievers.

The verse in Rom. 11:26 is based on Isa. 59:20-21 and 27:9. The fact is that "all" means "all," and this is confirmed in Heb. 8:11:

> ¹¹ And no longer will a man teach his neighbor, nor a man his brother, saying, "Know the Lord," because they will *all* know me, *from the least of them to the greatest*.

The landmark event in Biblical history took place when all believers entered the Promised Land. See Heb. 3:18-19:

> ¹⁸ And to whom did God swear that they would never enter his rest [land of Israel] if not to those who were disobedient? ¹⁹ And we see that they were not able to enter, because of their unbelief.

When the reader is equipped with an understanding of Semitic reasoning, one can easily see exaggerations in the text. There are multiple verses, which include or *imply* the words "all" and "no one" in the Bible. This is exactly what God said in His commandment in Deut. 10:19:

> ¹⁹ And you are to love those who are aliens, for you yourselves were aliens in Egypt.

The pages of the Bible reveal sarcasm in some statements of Jesus, and sometimes it is strong. Some commentaries explain the following verses as an analogy (Matt. 6:27):

> ²⁷ And who of you by worrying can add even one cubit to his life?

Time is not measured in cubits. This question cannot be answered, and it clearly sounds like mockery.

See Matt. 6:2:

> ² So when you give to the needy, do not sound a trumpet before you, as the hypocrites do in the synagogues and on the streets, to be honored by men...

The word "trumpet" here stands for a *shofar*, a lamb's horn, which is blown on *Yom Kippur*, the Day of Atonement. Believers pray for forgiveness of their sins committed through the past year. Hypocrites seek to help others to gain their own glorification, and call for attention.

See Mark 3:4:

> [4] And Jesus told them, "Which is lawful on the Sabbath: to do good or to do evil, to save life or to kill?" And they remained silent.

Jesus uses here *kal vachomer*. Since saving someone's life is a good deed and permissible even on Saturday, how much more all other good deeds are lawful and needed any time.

The comparison of Jews with Gentile unbelievers who worship idols is very unflattering and sarcastic. See Matt. 6:7:

> [7] And when you pray, do not keep on babbling like Gentiles, for they think they will be heard because of their many words.

See also Matt. 11:7:

> [7] And they went away, Jesus began to speak to the crowd about John: "What did you go out into the desert to see? A reed swayed by the wind?

Reeds did not grow in the places like Qasr el-Yahud, where John baptized. Besides, there were no swamps in this location. Currently the old minefield is there.

Several commonly used and incorrect interpretations may be found in Matt. 19:24-25:

> [24] And again I tell you, it is easier for a camel to go through the eye of a needle than for a rich man to enter the kingdom of God. [25] And when the disciples heard this, they were greatly astonished and asked, "Who then can be saved?"

The Jewish belief of the first century, that rich people are blessed by God with their wealth, is not Biblical. The categorical nature of this statement leads to the apparent impossibility of a rich person's salvation.

It turned out that many Bible readers do not concern themselves about the risk of being wealthy. They hope that the loving Lord will provide a small exception and let some rich people go to heaven. The story about a tiny wicket with the name "eye of a needle" through which a camel may be pulled with some difficulties[65] is invented by those who have never seen a wall of any fortress. But ordinary common sense suggests that the gate is the most vulnerable place of a fortress, so a gate's structural strength was never weakened by wickets. On the contrary, the gate is a very solid structure that withstands blows of a battering ram without damage. Moreover, the enemy would face a secondary gate after following an L-shaped turn.

But the text of the Gospel seems to leave no other explanation: the rich young man (Matt. 19:16-22), despite his outward behavior was not saved, and when faced with the problem of choosing between riches and salvation, chose against eternal life.[66] The same choice is made also by many supporters of the Prosperity Gospel.

The Bible does not make poverty a condition of salvation; rather, the *intention* toward personal wealth is the visible sign of disbelief. Thus, the implicit *kal vachomer* rule should be applied to the text in Matt. 19:24.

Culture and Environment

When and where was Jesus born? According to Church tradition, He was born in a stable manger in Bethlehem on December 25, 1 A.D. Tourists are brought to the Cave of the Nativity in the present day.

We will now take a closer look at the circumstances of this birth. There are no direct references to the date of His birth in the Bible, but there are some *indirect* ones.

Attempts have been made to analyze the length of service for the priest Zechariah in the Temple to determine the timing of the events in Luke 1:8-23, namely, by calculating the time of service of the priest Avia's

---

65 Cheryl Lynn Woolsey, My Best Friend Jesus (1998) 129; V. Gilbert Beers, What Everyone Should Know about the Bible (2007) 34.

66 Darrell L. Bock, Luke: the NIV application commentary from biblical text (1996) 468.

descendants in the Temple. But according to the Bible, descendants of Avia served in the Temple for one week twice a year. Meanwhile, all descendants of Aaron served as a group three times a year. In addition, every three or four years there is an extra month in the Jewish calendar: Adar Beit, the second Adar. Besides, the service in the Temple was interrupted twice for indefinite periods. Thus, no credible theory exists on the subject of the events of Luke 1:8-23 took place.

There is a common *incorrect* translation of *the only* verse regarding the event of Jesus' birth is in Luke 2:7:

> ⁷ And she gave birth to her firstborn, a son. And she wrapped him in cloths and placed him in a manger, because there was no room for them in the inn.

Since a manger belongs to a stable, offering a pregnant Jewish woman the place to deliver their baby next to the animals and their manure would have been a flagrant insult, followed by the revenge by relatives of the clan (up to 800 people). Besides, Matthew described the Magi as worshiping Jesus in a house, not a stable (Matt. 2:10-11):

> ¹⁰ When they saw the star, they were overwhelmed with joy. ¹¹ Entering the house, they saw the child with Mary his mother, and falling to their knees, they worshiped him...

A cave has also been suggested as the birthplace; however, the Jews did not use the caves as homes, they buried their dead in them.

The verse should be translated from Greek in the following way (Luke 2:7):

> ⁷ And she gave birth to her firstborn, a son. And she wrapped him in cloths and placed him in a *trough*, because there was no place for them in the *living quarters*.

This translation of word κατάλυμα is supported by Mark 14:14-15:

> ¹⁴ Say to the owner of the house he enters, "The Teacher asks: Where is my *guest room*, where I may eat the Passover with my disciples?" ¹⁵ He will show you a large upper room, furnished and ready...

See also Luke 22:11-12:

> [11] And say to the owner of the house, "The Teacher asks: Where is the *guest room*, where I may eat the Passover with my disciples?" [12] He will show you a large upper room, all furnished...

The extra feeding or watering trough would only be suitable for a baby if it were dry and clean, in which case it would be kept in a storeroom when not in use. Since the storage room is part of a house, it would be protected from elements of weather. When the labor began, the warm water and help of a midwife were needed.

Travelers usually prefer to stay with their relatives. Jesus' parents in Bethlehem in all likelihood might have relatives (Luke 1:39-50, 2:3-4), and it was common for relatives to offer hospitality. They would perceive refusal to stay with them as an insult. To be in the neighborhood and not visit their extended family relatives would be a very short-sighted decision. Moreover, Joseph and Miryam (Mary) were young and very poor (Luke 2:24):

> [24] And to offer a sacrifice in keeping with what is said in the Law of the Lord: "a pair of doves or two young pigeons."

This was the cheapest sacrifice allowed in the Temple.

See Luke 2:41:

> [41] Every year his parents went to Jerusalem for the Feast of the Pesach.

The three great Jewish pilgrimage festivals (Pesach, Shavuot, Sukkot) were originally celebrated in Jerusalem with sacrifices and Temple worship (Ex. 23:14-17, 34:23-24, Lev. 23, Deut. 16:16). During these festivals the number of people in Jerusalem increased fivefold. All possible room were occupied in the city, and the poorest pilgrims looked for shelter outside the city walls. Bethlehem was located an almost three-hour walk from Jerusalem, and thus it is possible that Jesus' parents decided to combine their visit to the Temple for the feast with their participation in the census ordered by Caesar Augustus that year.

Their journey likely took more time due to Miryam's (Mary) pregnancy, and they might have arrived in Bethlehem just before the feast. Some researchers suggest that the date might be in the spring of 6 B.C., 4 Nisan (March 3). The timing is not in conflict with the shepherds in the field this season (Luke 2:8).

In general, this was an ordinary delivery of an extraordinary child.

See Luke 11:5-7:

> [5] And he said to them, "Suppose one of you has a friend, and he goes to him at midnight and says, 'Friend, lend me three loaves of bread, [6] because a friend of mine on a journey has come to me, and I have nothing to set before him.' [7] And the one inside answers, saying, 'Don't bother me. The door is already locked, and my children are with me in bed. I can't get up and give you the bread.'"

Two thousand years ago, people did not travel at night or alone in this area. There were two reasons: a single traveler could have been robbed or even killed in a robbery, or could have been captured and sold into slavery (Luke 10:30).

Therefore, people traveled in groups for protection from individual robbers and small local gangs. Since the group's security depends on good visibility, and Israel is a mountainous country, a group will usually have camps overnight with posted guards. In addition, traveling at night through rugged mountain terrain takes more time.

The summer heat brings its own adjustments to the daily routine, a break for the afternoon siesta. The journey itself is slow, and it could have taken up to seven hours per day after that. Major roads had caravanserais for needed rest for people and animals. One could spend the night under protection of walls and stock up food and water for the next day of journey. In winter, the rains pour in Israel, *wadi*[57] are filled with water and the pace of travel slows down.

Thus, the arrival of travelers in the middle of the night was unusual. Apparently, they were delayed on the road because of some unforeseen circumstances.

---

57 The rivers that dry up in the summer.

In ancient times, small buns of bread were baked only for the rich. It is reasonable to assume that a loaf weighed about two pounds. Three loaves should have fed a dozen people; thus, the friend came from the road with a group of people.

In order for a neighbor to get the door opened, he has to scream and knock. Therefore, he woke up everybody in the house, and the owner's explanations sounds like an excuse. He changed his mind only when he realized that he and his household would not sleep that night. The story itself illustrates the contrast between this man's reaction and God's response to calls for any help.

Middle Eastern Customs

There are also various customs in the Middle East (continuing into today, in some cases) that add more depth to the Biblical account. There was a case when an American military car was driving in Baghdad. The soldiers would see shopkeepers sitting along the road, lifting their feet to demonstrate dirty soles of their shoes, which is a very rude Middle Eastern insult.

Knowledge of the local customs in the Middle East comes in handy in Mark 6:11:

> [11] And if any place will not welcome you or listen to you, shake the dust off your feet when you leave, as a testimony against them.

Jesus was uncompromising towards the unbelievers.

The student of the Bible can find advice on kissing (Ps. 85:10):

> [10] Love and faithfulness meet together; righteousness and peace kiss each other.

Righteousness and peace are masculine nouns in Hebrew, but as they are concepts and not humans, they cannot kiss. In the Middle East, a kiss is all about friendliness.

See Matt. 26:48-49:

> [48] And he who was betraying Him gave them a sign, saying, "The

one I kiss is the man; take him." [49] Going at once to Jesus, Judas said, "Shalom, Rabbi!" and kissed him.

The Gospel stresses that the symbol of friendship was used for the evil purpose of betrayal.

In Rom. 16:16 Paul gives advice:

[16] Greet one another with a holy kiss.

The same advice was given in 1 Cor. 16:20, 2 Cor. 13:12, 1 Thess. 5:26, and 1 Peter 5:14. It is not noticeable in translation that the word "one another" is a *masculine* expression. This custom did not apply to females. The Greek men who attended these Churches used the Greek custom of shaking hands instead of the Jewish custom to kiss.

We will find the expression "to speak with mouth to mouth" in the Bible, for example, in Jer. 34:3:

[3] You will not escape from his grasp but will surely be captured and handed over to him. You will see the king of Babylon with your own eyes, and he will speak with you *mouth to mouth*.

In the Middle East people talk at a close distance of 1.5 ft. or less, so this is a very accurate description.

See 2 John 12:

[12] I have much to write to you, but I do not want to use paper and ink. Instead, I hope to visit you and talk with your *mouth to mouth*, so that our joy may be complete.

See also 3 John 14:

[14] I hope to see you soon, and we will talk *mouth to mouth*.

On birds and the Temple, see Mark 11:15:

[15] And they came to Jerusalem, And Jesus entered the Temple area and began driving out those who were buying and selling in the Temple. And he overturned the tables of the money changers and the benches of those selling doves.

Poor people may sacrifice two pigeons, but birds near the Temple would have cost four times as much.

Some commentators[68] suggest the following:

> When Jesus arrived in Jerusalem, He went into the temple area, the large outer court of the Gentiles surrounding the inner sacred courts of the temple itself. Jesus was outraged by this blatant disregard for the temple area specifically set apart for Gentile use.

Many commentators place the money-changers in the Temple, in the courtyard of the Gentiles, which leads to the desecration of the Temple. However, the Talmud preserved the knowledge about the ban on any trade activity within the Temple, *including* the court of the Gentiles. People were prohibited even to enter with a money bag into the Temple courts.

Besides, regular Roman coins were not allowed in the Temple, as the portraits of Roman emperors were minted on them. According to Jewish Law it was forbidden to bring graven images in the Temple. Exchange places were used to change non-kosher money for coins without people's images. These coins were issued during the uprising of Bar Kohba in the second century A.D. Even today Israeli coins do not have images of people.

Thus, the money-changers had to be in the area adjacent to the Temple, as the priests did not allow it in the Temple. Money-changers could trade on the stairs leading to the Temple, or next to the stairs, under Robinson's Arch. However, these places were clearly outside of the Temple. When Herod the Great rebuilt the Temple, he turned a fairly small peak of a steep mountain into a larger area, where a massive amount of dirt was used to increase and level the Temple courts, though it was not made completely flat. The current almost-flat plaza was completed by the Turks during the reign of Suleiman the Magnificent between 1537 and 1541. It is clearly seen today in the upper part of the western wall. The Turks used stones that weighed only half a ton while Herod's huge stones weighed up to ten tons. Thus, during the reign of Herod, the Temple Square was still shaped like a hump.

---

68 John F. Walvoord, Roy B. Zuck, The Bible Knowledge Commentary (1983).

In order to reduce construction costs and the amount of work needed, inner cavities were left inside the Temple mound. The mound itself was extended to the south, as it is seen by the seam on the eastern wall of the Temple Mount.

One of these cavities has been excavated by archaeologists and is known as the "Solomon's stables," although the place itself has nothing to do with Solomon. This section is 83 ft x 197 ft, and can be accessed from the outside by a staircase, with another staircase leading up to the Temple square. Thus, Solomon's stables were not part of the Temple, but were under the Temple square inside the Temple mound.[69]

People came there by so called "pilgrim's road", the widest street in Jerusalem (25 feet), which ran from Siloam pool to the Huldah Gates (1800 feet). Some underground vaulted tunnels lead to the Temple Mount and "Solomon's stables". All "pilgrim's road" was sided by shops where people could buy everything needed for the Temple visit.

The words of Jesus, "And you have made it a den of robbers," fit the description of Solomon's stables remarkably well. It is easy to imagine the cave with overturned tables and scattered coins on the floor. Since 1996, Solomon's stables have been rebuilt into El-Marwani Mosque. In the process of construction, the part of the Herod's southern wall was destroyed and replaced by a patch of stones significantly lighter in color. This transformation of Solomon's stables into a mosque was meant to "prove" the "triumph" of Islam over Judaism.

See 2 Sam. 11:2:

> [2] And it came to pass one evening David got up from his bed and walked around on the roof of the palace. And from the roof he saw a woman bathing. And the woman was very beautiful.

People used to rest on flat rooftops in the Middle East in the warm evenings. The royal palace was on top of the mountain, where there was no place for other houses. The slope below was steep, so that David looked at the woman almost from the top down, where everything was perfectly visible. Of course, BatSheva knew all of this when she chose

69 It could be also vestibule in double passage under Al Aksa or triple gates passages, see Captain W. Charles Wilson R.E., Ordnance Survey of Jerusalem (1865) 167.

the space and time for her bath; as was expected, David understood the invitation and accepted it. Both of them broke the Law.

Common Sense

See Prov. 3:21, 23-24:

> [21] Maintain sound wisdom and discretion. My son, don't lose sight of them...
> [23] Then you will go safely on your way; your foot will not stumble.
> [24] When you lie down, you will not be afraid; you will lie down, and your sleep will be pleasant.

The combination of wisdom and discretion is critical while reading and interpreting the Bible.

Take, for example, one of the most commonly quoted passages in the Bible (John 3:16):

> [16] And God so loved the world that he gave his one and only Son, that whoever believes in him shall not perish but have eternal life.

The words "one and only Son" are difficult to understand in the light of the Nicaea symbol of faith.[70] The language of John is straightforward: Jesus was conceived by God, born, lived, died, and rose again, and all of this applies only to the human nature of Jesus.

Jesus, Yeshua in Hebrew, called himself a "son of man," which corresponds to the Hebrew idiom "son of Adam" or a man. The Hebrew word "son" has several meanings and means not only a son in the literal sense, but also a descendant or a part of some group, as in the expression "son of punishment" (Deut. 25:2):

> [2] And it shall be, if the wicked man is *son of punishment*, that the judge shall cause him to lie down, and to be beaten before his face.

Apostle Paul in 1 Cor. 15:22, 45 uses the Hebrew wordplay of Adam and "son of Adam" to build a contrast between sin/death and faith/life. Paul continued this theme in Rom. 5:14, calling Adam a type of

---

70 C. T. R. Hewer, Understanding Islam: an introduction (2006) 180.

the Coming One, and he uses the rule *kal vachomer* six times in Rom. 5:15-21.

Common sense can work to enact Occam's razor; the simplest and most obvious reading often makes it easy to choose the correct explanation for any text, which can then be tested for contradictions with the entire text of the Bible.

Golem

Golem is a Hebrew word found only once in the Bible (Ps. 139:16):

> [16] Your eyes saw my unformed body. All the days ordained for me were written in your book before one of them came to be.

The word *golem* stands here for an unformed substance such as clay that will be endowed with life in the future. In the Talmud, Sanhedrin 38b, Adam is described as initially a *golem* (גֹּלֶם) while his dust was "kneaded into a shapeless husk."

Another passage confirms the concept of *golem* (Ex. 21:22-25):

> [22] And *if* men struggle with each other and strike a woman with child so that she has a miscarriage, yet there is no *further* injury, he shall surely be fined as the woman's husband may demand of him; and he shall pay as the judges *decide*. [23] But if there is *any further* injury, then you shall appoint *as a penalty* life for life, [24] eye for eye, tooth for tooth, hand for hand, foot for foot, [25] burn for burn, wound for wound, bruise for bruise.

In certain cases, the rule of equal retribution cannot be applied because of the differences between male and female physiology; only equal physical harm to the woman requires the use of equal retaliation.

Modern science is completely in agreement with the Bible. Monozygotic (identical) twins are the result of the same single conception when one group of cells splits in two or more groups with the same DNA. Another example is presented by tetragametic chimerism when two genetically distinct conspecific individuals fuse together generating the single entity, or multiple conceptions merge with only one human body with multiple DNA. By the way, the brindle animals are chimeras too.

Life

The Bible defines the source of human life in Gen. 2:7:

> ⁷ And the LORD God formed man *of* the dust of the ground and breathed into his nostrils the breath of life; and man became a soul alive [*nefesh haya*].

Thus, God's breath in the nostrils has produced life. This was accepted as the definition of life in the era before modern science. Death as the lack of breath is described in Gen. 6:17:

> ¹⁷ ...I do bring a flood of waters upon the earth to destroy all flesh, wherein the breath of life; everything that on the earth shall die.

The statement was repeated in many other verses, e.g., Job 27:3:

> ³ as long as my breath is still in me and the breath from God remains in my nostrils,

The breath of God even gives life to the Scriptures (2 Tim. 3:16):

> ¹⁶ All Scripture is God-breathed and is profitable for teaching, for rebuking, for correcting, for training in righteousness...

Even the dead could be made alive by the God's breath (Ezek. 37:4-5):

> ⁴ Then he said to me, "Prophesy to these bones and say to them, 'Dry bones, hear the word of the Lord! ⁵ This is what the Sovereign Lord says to these bones: I will make breath (*ruah*) enter you, and you will come to life."

The New Testament brings another description of the process of raising from dead (Rev. 11:11):

> ¹¹ But after the three and a half days a breath of life from God entered them, and they stood on their feet.

Human life starts with the first breath, life of the believer starts with God's breath (John 20:22).

The Torn Curtain in the Temple

See Mark 15:38:

> [38] And the curtain of the Temple was torn in two from top to bottom.

It is generally believed that this curtain separated two rooms, the Holy Place and Holy of Holies in the Temple in the time of Jesus. This space was called *devir*, translated as "inner sanctuary" in 1 Kings 6:19-22. Once a year, on the Day of Atonement, the High Priest went through the barrier between God's holy presence and the sinful world to offer the blood sacrifice and incense.

Some commentators interpret Mark 15:38 on the tear becoming the symbol of open access to God from now on.[71] This interpretation leads to the allegation that the Covenant between God and Israel was abrogated.[72] The narration of the Bible, however, is at odds with this explanation. More importantly, it does not support the description of the Second Temple interior.

The drapes and curtains were needed in the tabernacle or the tent of meeting because it was a transportable structure (Ex. 26:31-34). With the construction of Solomon's Temple, the walls of the Holy of Holies were ostensibly lined with twenty-three tons of gold, and the curtains were replaced by doors of substantial size (1 Kings 6:31-35). As described by Joseph Flavius,[73] the inner door was allegedly eighty-two feet high, seven yards wide, and about fifteen tons in weight. According to other reports, there were *two* curtains in front of that door.[74]

In the time of the Second Temple, built in 516 B.C., the Holy of Holies no longer contained the Ark of the Covenant. However, the large stone, called the foundation stone, on which the Ark was placed in the time of the First Temple was there. And no commentaries exist regarding the cave[75] that was under the floor of the Holy of Holies, as well as the

---

71 Daniel M. Gurtner, The torn veil: Matthew's exposition of the death of Jesus (2007) 44-46.

72 The New American Bible (2005) 1060; Warren W. Wiersbe, The Bible exposition commentary: Volume 1 (2003) 103.

73 Margaret Barker, The great high priest: the temple roots of Christian liturgy (2003) 146.

74 Mishnah, Yoma 5.2; Mishna, Middoth, mishnah 1.

75 Andreas Kaplony, The Haram of Jerusalem, 324-1099: temple, Friday Mosque, area of spiritual power (2002) 753-754.

round slab cover on the floor of the cave, and what was hidden under that slab. We can find a reference to the cave from Captain Montague Parker, fifth Earl of Morley, who on April 17, 1911, entered the Dome of the Rock surreptitiously and began to search for gold. This Islamic shrine was built on the site of Second Temple in 692 A.D.

In any case, it is not possible today to establish exactly where this torn curtain was located. But it is certain that the access to the Holy of Holies remained closed on the day of crucifixion, because it was open only on the Day of Atonement. The heavy curtain might have hung across the door of the inner sanctuary, separating the priests from all worshippers. In all likelihood, when the free-hanging fabric was ripped from top to bottom, but the structure of the building was not damaged, it could be seen as the miracle.

In this case, having some common knowledge about the Middle East would be of help to commentators. The tear of the cloth was an expression of the deepest grief. The Torah commands to tear one's clothes (usually it is a tear from the neck down) as a sign of mourning. The curtain torn in the Temple should be perceived as the sign to the Jews that God was grieving for Jesus.

Letter to the Disobedient Church

Letter to the Romans

Paul's Letter to the Romans is one of the least understood and most misinterpreted books of the New Testament. *Obedience* is the key word in this letter, and it is found in Rom. 1:5-6, 8:7, 13:1, 15:18, 16:19, and 16:26.

In analyzing Romans, it is critical to study two theological themes: the position of Jewish and Gentile believers toward God, and their position within the Church. Nowadays, these themes, and the second one in particular, are frequently interpreted with a bias.

While Paul was called by God to be "an apostle to the Gentiles" in Acts 9:15, he always stopped in a local synagogue in a new city first (Acts 13:14, 14:1, 17:1-2, 17:10, 17:16-17, 18:4, 18:9, 19:8, 28:17).

Paul reasons with the Semitic question-response pattern. Many contemporary commentators do not define the *primary* purpose of the text of Romans. They single out the preparation for Paul's planned visit to Rome on the way to Spain (Rom. 1:13, 15:22-24, 28), or mention the need to minister to the believers in Rome.[76] However, Paul designates 97% of his letter to a different theme.

Paul declares his goal in the key part of the epistle (Rom. 15:1-2, 5-7, 10):

> [1] We who are strong ought to bear with the failings of the weak and not to please ourselves. [2] Each of us should please his neighbor for his good, to build him up...
> [5] May the God who gives endurance and encouragement give you a spirit of unity among yourselves as you follow Christ Jesus, [6] so that with one heart and mouth you may glorify the God and Father of our Lord Jesus Christ. [7] Accept one another, then, just as Christ accepted you, in order to bring praise to God...
> [10] Again, it says, "Rejoice, O Gentiles, with his people."

Here are two examples of well-known theological reasoning which is in contrast to Pauline teaching to the Roman Christians. As early as the fourth century, Augustine taught that the Jews bear the mark of Cain because they are Christ killers:

> 11. Then God says to Cain: "You are cursed from the earth, which has opened its mouth to receive your brother's blood at your hand." 12 ...The continued preservation of the Jews will be a proof to believing Christians of the subjection merited by those who, in the pride of their kingdom, put the Lord to death.
> 13 ...Only when a Jew comes over to Christ, he is no longer Cain.[77]

Karl Barth, the famous Swiss theologian of the twentieth century, stated that Jewish believers and the Church are not part of Israel: "Israel is the people of the Jews which resists its election; the Church is the gathering of Jews and Gentiles called on the ground of its election."[78]

[76] Colin G. Kruse, Paul's Letter to the Romans (2012) 10-11.

[77] Contra Faustum, Book XII, by St. Augustine, 398.

[78] Karl Barth. Church Dogmatics Volume 2.2 The Doctrine of God (1957) 365.

"The election of Israel, then, is not only negatively confirmed by the fact that Israel as such and as a whole has in any case to fulfill its determination and to serve as a reflection of the divine judgment."[79]

Christianity in Rome emerged from within the Jewish community (Acts 2:10), and the Letter to the Romans is dominated by the issue of Jew/Gentile relationships. Jews were banished from Rome by Emperor Claudius's edict in 49 A.D.; they were able to come back four years later after the emperor's death. Upon arrival, the Jews found that Gentile Christians did not desire to share the leadership positions in the Church. Moreover, they demanded that Jewish believers, their brothers and sisters in faith, stop observing all Jewish customs.

For Paul, who accepted the Nazirite vow (Acts 11:20-26) and kept the Law of Moses without a blemish, that teaching was unacceptable. Paul attributed those tensions and teachings to satanic temptations (Rom. 16:20). Thus, he wrote the Epistle, which required considerable expense in terms of time and materials.

The Epistle is much more than a conventional letter.[80] It often sounds like an accusatory speech of a prosecutor, or a prosecutor's argumentation.

The best way to understand the letter is to start with Rom. 16, which contains many clues for the reader.

In Rom. 1:1-7 Paul presents himself and names Gentile believers in the Church as his addressees and reminds them about "*obedience* of faith" (Rom. 1:5). Addressing them as saints, Paul embraces them as fellow heirs in the mission and those "set apart" for God. Thus, this Roman Church faced a conflict which was deemed to be resolved.

Paul lays out his reasoning in Rom. 1:16: "salvation of everyone who believes: *firstly, to the Jew, and also to the Gentile.*" The use of the Greek word *proton* without enumeration implies priority and may be translated as "first by importance." Paul uses the word "Greek" synonymously with the word "Gentile." He tied this goal to the evangelism

---

79 Karl Barth. Church Dogmatics Volume 2.2 The Doctrine of God (1957) 544

80 Lung, Kwong Lo, Paul's purpose in writing Romans: The upbuilding of a Jewish and gentile Christian community in Rome, Doctoral thesis, Durham University (1988) 17-21.

of the Jewish people based on their *covenantal* priority.

Paul uses the word *proton* again in Rom. 2:9-10:

> [9] There will be trouble and distress for every human being who does evil: *firstly, to the Jew, and also to the Gentile,* [10] but glory, honor and peace for everyone who does good: *firstly, to the Jew, and also to the Gentile.*

We find the second principle in Rom. 2:13: "And the hearers of the law are not righteous before God, but the doers of the law will be justified." Generally, Rom. 2:12-29 maintains that Jews and Gentiles are equally responsible for keeping or breaking the Law.

In chapter 3 Paul describes multiple benefits of being Jewish and reasons referring to the Bible and applying *gezera shava*. The Gentiles in the Roman Church could understand the rule's logic only if they looked for help from the Jewish believers.

In Rom. 3:20 Paul teaches that "the knowledge of sin comes through the Law." He follows by affirming that faith upholds the Law (Rom. 3:27-28); Rom. 3:20 presents the expression "works of the law [without faith]."

Because Paul frequently uses the implicit rule of *gezera shava* and sometimes quotes the Bible out of context, as in Rom. 3:10-18, the reader might get confused. Understanding this rule helps us to differentiate applications of the word "Law." For example, see Rom. 3:20:

> [20] For no one will be justified in his sight by the works of the Law [of works], because the knowledge of sin comes through the Law.

See also Rom. 7:6, 22-23:

> [6] And now we have been released from the Law [of works], since we have died to what held us, so that we may serve in the newness of the Spirit and not in the old letter of the Law [of works]...
> [22] And in my inner being I delight in God's Law; [23] and I see another Law [of works] at work in the members of my body, waging war against the Law of my mind and making me a prisoner of the Law [of works] of sin at work within my members.

In chapter 4, Paul states that Abraham is righteous because of his faith. Paul stresses the word "accounted," citing Gen. 15:6 in Rom. 4:3. In Rom. 4:6-8 he refers to Ps. 32:1-2 (LXX) and points out that "accounting" in the Psalms is founded on God's grace. Gentile believers are also righteous because of their faith in Lord Jesus Christ. Paul uses *gezera shava* when he declares them to be descendants of Abraham in Rom. 4:11-12.

Paul delivers the argument using *kal vachomer* in Rom. 5:9-21, where he draws a comparison between Adam and Jesus, both of whom performed an action that had consequences for the entire human race. Paul's presentation of the act of disobedience versus the act of obedience provides the proper backdrop for dealing with the disobedient congregation.

In the beginning of the Rom. 6, Paul elaborates on the answer to the question he posed in Rom. 3:8; we find his answer in Rom. 6:6. Paul emphasizes life, righteousness, and grace as victory over sin and death. Believers struggle against and defeat their old nature.

In chapter 7, Paul continues to bring clarity regarding the Law. He writes about the struggle with old nature using a diatribe style of reasoning. The Law shows God's requirements, exposes the sin, and the Law (of works) produces death in Rom. 7:9-13.

Chapter 8 begins with "no condemnation for those who are in Christ Jesus" and ends with no separation "from the love of God that is in Christ Jesus." In Rom. 8:11, Paul writes that the body is still under a death sentence. God indwells believers with the Spirit who ultimately will resurrect their bodies. In Rom. 8:15, where he writes "you received the Spirit of adoption," Paul teaches about Gentile believers' adoption into Israel. It was included by God in the Moab Covenant (Deut. 29:10-15). In the period before writing to the Romans Paul referred to it in 1 Cor. 12:2:

> [2] You know that when you *were* Gentiles...

After writing to the Romans, Paul stated the following in Eph. 2:11, 19:

[11] Therefore, remember that *formerly* you who are Gentiles...

[19] And you are *no longer* foreigners and aliens...

In Rom. 8:28-30 he defends the predestination of believers.

Rom 9-11 constitutes a special unit within the Epistle with a focus on both groups of believers and their interface and positions in faith. These chapters are truly critical for equipping the Church to carry out the mission of Jewish evangelism and require careful attention. Since the New Covenant is made with Israel (Jer. 31:31), Paul's teaching is aligned with all authors of the New Testament as well as Jesus' teaching.

While expounding on Israel's election as God's people from Abraham all the way down to Jesus' followers, Paul teaches that Gentile believers become part of Israel based on their faith in the Jewish Messiah. Their rights and their responsibilities follow from this inclusion.

These chapters cover the natural progression of Israel from the past to the future.

With chapter 9, Paul focuses his attention on the problem of the Roman Church. Being heartbroken, he states that he would give up his own salvation for the sake of his Jewish brethren (Rom. 9:1-4). Christ is the pinnacle of all God's promises (Rom. 9:4-5). God operates on the basis of sovereign election. The word and promises of God have not failed, since they were intended for the faithful remnant within the nation of Israel as a whole (Rom. 9:6-7).

All Semitic people in ancient times followed the law of primogeniture, where the firstborn male had the right of succession and inheritance. Contrary to this law the second child, Jacob, as the child of the promise, was elected by God before his birth (Rom. 9:11-13).

God was not done with the people of Israel, having patience while molding the nation. Instead of discarding the clay of it, He reshaped Israel, including Gentiles within the nation (Rom. 9:20-26). Paul completes the chapter by writing that Israel stumbled, but did not fail (Rom. 9:30-33).

Paul shares his prayers for Israel to be saved (Rom. 10:1), emphasizing that Israel pursues righteousness by works. He contrasts self-righteousness with submission to God's righteousness. In Rom. 10:12 he says that "there is no distinction between Jew and Greek" implying that the division in the Church should not take place. Paul expounds Deut. 30:14 on the message of faith in the believer's mouth and heart, which must be reflected in his life. In Rom. 10:14-15 he calls Gentile believers to Jewish evangelism once more. Their faith and lives will make Jews envious (Rom. 10:19-21). The "nation without understanding" in v. 19 is better translated from Deut. 32:21 as "nation of Gentiles."

Paul continues to make his case that God did not cast off His people in Rom. 11:1-5. The Elijah story indicates that the remnant avoided idolatry even at the time of deepest apostasy (1 Kings 19:18).

Rom. 11:11-27 supports the Biblical mandate for Gentiles to be taken into the body of the Messiah, and to reach the Jewish people with the Gospel message. The most effective way to engage in Jewish evangelism is to provoke them to jealousy (Rom. 11:11). The Jewish people would see God's light shine through Christians, their close relationship with Him, and the blessings coming upon those who have believed in God of Israel through Jesus. The Lord will evaluate either success or failure to make Israel jealous.

The analogy of the olive tree confirms how Gentile believers relate to Israel. It is easy to understand confusion in the Church on this issue due to the common mistranslation of Rom. 11:17-21:

> [17] And if some of the branches have been broken off, and you, though a wild olive shoot, have been grafted in *among them* and now share in the nourishing sap from the olive root, [18] do not boast over those branches. And if you do, consider this: You do not support the root, but the root supports you. [19] And you will say then, "Branches were broken off so that I could be grafted in." [20]Granted. But they were broken off because of unbelief, and you stand by faith. Do not be arrogant, but be afraid. [21] And if God did not spare the natural branches, he will not spare you either.

The translations found in the NAB, CEV, NRSV, RSV, GWT, ISV,

NCB, and non-English translations typically read v. 17 as "grafted in *instead of them.*"

This departure from the original text would justify Replacement Theology, or supersessionism. These types of mistranslations might lead believers to disobey Biblical teaching which in turn delays the prophecy's fulfillment in Rom. 11:25-27:

> [25] And I do not want you to be ignorant of this mystery, brothers, so that you may not be conceited: Israel has experienced a hardening in part until the full number of the Gentiles has come in. [26] And so all Israel will be saved, as it is written: "The deliverer will come from Zion; and he will turn godlessness away from Jacob. [27] And this is my Covenant with them when I take away their sins."

These verses show that the faith of Jews and Gentile Christians are inextricably linked. By way of partial blindness on the part of the Jews, the believing Gentiles were brought in and called to provoke Israel to jealousy. God's plan includes salvation and fullness of the nations. He is still building "His household." "All Israel" represents the corporate Israel in her completeness at the time of the Messiah's second coming.

Without the Jewish people, the Church is not connected to the foundation of Israel's destiny. The Gentile believers are grafted into the olive tree, bearing the fruits and partaking in sap from the root system. God is faithful to His covenant with Israel's forefathers (Deut. 7:8). The nation as a whole will return to join Jewish and Gentile believers as a recipient of mercy (Rom. 11:28-29):

> [28] As far as *election* is concerned, and they [Jews] are loved on account of the patriarchs, [29] and God's gifts and his call are *irrevocable*.

Paul has laid the groundwork for reconciliation in the Roman Church in chapters 1-11. In chapter 12 he provides the practical counsel to Gentile believers to be drawn out from his Jewish perspective. The Apostle refers to the will of God defined in the Old Testament, and states that Israel should repent and live in faith (Rom. 12:1-2). Paul charged Gentile and Jewish believers to live in harmony with one another in Rom. 12:16. He used implicit rule *kal vachomer* in Rom. 12:9-13, Rom. 12:20, and most notably in Rom. 12:18:

> [18] If it is possible, as far as it depends on you, live at peace with everyone.

Thus, *how much more* do Gentile believers need to be at peace with their Jewish brothers in the same Church.

In the Roman Empire, citizens did not pay taxes but could be conscripted into the army. Only the non-citizens, including manumitted slaves, were taxed. Paul applies the implicit *kal vachomer* teaching that, if his addressees obey the Roman authorities, *how much more* should they obey Paul's authority.

In Rom. 13:8-14, he tells Gentile believers to keep commandments of the Law. Paul stresses the commandment to love one's neighbor, which summarizes God's Law and is always referred to in Judaism. Paul concludes with calling the Roman Church to righteous conduct by "clothing" themselves in Jesus. This image of putting on righteousness is found in Isa. 61:10, as well as Job 29:14:

> [14] I put on righteousness, and it clothed me; My justice was like a robe and a turban.

Chapters 14-15:13 contain the central point of the Epistle and should be interpreted within the context of Gentile-Jewish discord in their Roman congregation. The focal point of contention was the Jewish way of life and keeping the Law of Moses. It is important to note that Paul appears to reconcile only one side in the conflict, as he did not give any advice to Jewish believers.

Chapter 14 continues to call the Roman Church to abandon judgment and reconcile, lest the weak (Jewish believers) leave the faith and unbelieving Jews would not accept their Messiah (Rom. 14:1-3, 6, 13-16, 21):

> [1] And accept him whose faith is weak, without passing judgment on disputable matters. [2] One man's faith allows him to eat everything, but another man, whose faith is weak, eats only vegetables. [3] The man who eats everything must not look down on him who

does not, and the man who does not eat everything must not condemn the man who does, for God has accepted him...

⁶ He who regards one day as special, does so to the Lord. He who eats meat, eats to the Lord, and he gives thanks to God; and he who abstains, does so to the Lord and gives thanks to God...

¹³ And let us stop passing judgment on one another. Instead, make up your mind not to put any stumbling block or obstacle in your brother's way. ¹⁴ And as one who is in the Lord Jesus, I am fully convinced that no food is unclean in itself. If anyone regards something as unclean, then for him it is unclean. ¹⁵ And if your brother is distressed because of what you eat, you are no longer acting in love. Do not by your eating destroy your brother for whom Christ died. ¹⁶ Do not allow what you consider good to be spoken of as evil...

²¹ It is better not to eat meat or drink wine or to do anything else that will cause your brother to fall.

Paul mentions the unclean (non-kosher) food in v. 14. In v. 21, Paul advises Gentile believers how the problem could be solved while they share meals. The presence of a relatively large Jewish community in Rome tells us that Gentile Christians would not have any real difficulty in procuring kosher meat and wine, if they so desired. If Gentile believers wanted to compromise, they could have served different meals for Gentile and Jewish believers while breaking bread in the fellowship. Besides, vegetables could be eaten in any circumstances (Rom. 14:2).

Paul advises regarding a similar conflict (1 Cor 8:9-13):

⁹ And be careful, however, that the exercise of your freedom does not become a stumbling block to the weak. ¹⁰ And if anyone with a weak conscience sees you who have this knowledge eating in an idol's temple, won't he be emboldened to eat what has been sacrificed to idols? ¹¹ And this weak brother, for whom Christ died, is destroyed by your knowledge. ¹² And when you sin against your brothers in this way and wound their weak conscience, you sin against Christ. ¹³ Therefore, if what I eat causes my brother to fall into sin, I will never eat meat again, so that I will not cause him to fall.

He continues (1 Cor. 10:31-32):

> [31] So whether you eat or drink or whatever you do, do it all for the glory of God. [32] Do not cause anyone to stumble, whether Jews, Greeks or the church of God.

The believers in the Roman Church could have known about this letter. Moreover, Paul's Jewish friends in Rome would be of help in resolving the conflict.

Paul specifies the unwillingness of Gentile believers in the Roman Church to solve the conflict. He uses words ὀφείλω, "pay off a *legal debt*" and ἀρέσκω, "satisfy" to charge Gentile believers in egotism contrary to teaching of Jesus (Rom. 15:1-3):

> [1] And we who are strong *indebted* to bear the weaknesses of those without strength, and not to *satisfy* ourselves. [2] Each one of us is to please his neighbor for his good, to build him up. [3] And even Christ did not please himself...

He calls the Romans to emulate their Lord Jesus, who served and edified. Paul quotes the Messianic text of Ps. 69, that predicts the suffering of Messiah hundreds of years before His birth (Rom. 15:3).

Paul also teaches on the intensive family relationship within the Church (Rom. 15:5-7):

> [5] And the God who gives endurance and encouragement may give you to live in harmony with one another according to Christ Jesus, [6] so that with *one mind and mouth* you may glorify the God and Father of our Lord Jesus Christ. [7] *Strongly welcome one another*, then, just as Christ accepted you, in order to glory of God.

Paul charges Gentile believers to unite with the Jewish brothers. The expression "His nation" is used only when referring to Israel in the Scriptures (Rom. 15:10-12):

> [10] And again, it says, "Rejoice, Gentiles, with His nation." [11] And again, "Praise the Lord, all Gentiles, and praises to him, all peoples." [12] And again, Isaiah says, "The Root of Jesse will spring up,

one who will arise to rule over the Gentiles; the Gentiles will hope in him."

Quotations from Deut. 32:43 in Rom. 15:10 and from Isa. 11:10 in Rom. 15:12 are given from the Septuagint, and not from the Hebrew text.

In Rom. 15:18 Paul confirms that his purpose is "to lead the Gentiles to obey God."

The following story conveys a very different outcome in a mainline Christian denomination, which acted contrary to Paul's teaching. The Messianic Jewish congregation Avodat Yisrael was established by the Presbytery of Philadelphia and opened its doors in 2003. Presbyterian officials insisted that the congregation would not evangelize the Jews (in contradiction to the Biblical teaching) and would not advertise its presence. In eighteen months, the Presbytery cut off funding on the basis of the congregation's failure to attract new members and the lack of growth. One year later, the General Assembly of the Presbyterian Church (USA) authorized the start of the Boycott, Divestment and Sanctions movement against Israel. The number of Jewish believers in the Presbyterian Church (USA) decreased as a result of the "experiment."

In 2014 the Presbyterian Church (USA) published its "Zionism Unsettled, a congregational study guide" which the Anti-Defamation League immediately declared "the most anti-Semitic document to come out of a mainline American church in recent memory."

Paul sent his greetings through the addressees to Christians in other Roman congregations (Rom. 16:3-16). According to some Biblical expositors a quarter of the names listed here belong to Jews. Jewish catacombs in Rome with thousands of tombs have inscriptions which reveal the names of up to thirteen synagogues, where roughly 85% of the recorded personal names are Latin or Greek.[81] If we take into account that a significant proportion of Jews acquired Roman names, then it might be one-third or more Jews who received these greetings. If we take into account that only 15% of Jews had Jewish names, then

81 Leon, Harry J. The Jews of Ancient Rome (1960).

all addressees in Rom. 16 were Jewish.

Paul could have greeted other believers directly. His intention was that the addressees would personally meet the believers (many of whom were Jewish) and his friends from other Roman congregations who might be mediators and advisers in the current conflict.

Paul words of admonishment are to be on guard against those in their midst who would cause strife and divisions, and promote false teachings for self-profit within the body (Rom. 16:17-18, 20):

> [17] And I urge you, brothers and sisters, to watch out for those who create divisions and obstacles contrary to the teaching that you learned and turn away from them, [18] and such do not serve our Lord Christ but their own belly, and they deceive the hearts of the innocents with smooth talk and flattery...
> [20] And the God of peace will quickly crush Satan under your feet...

Conclusion

It is known from history that the Church eventually developed theologies to defend the ideas of the Church in Rome by opposing Apostles Paul and Peter.

Later the Second Council of Nicaea (787 A.D.) severed the ties between Judaism and Christianity. We read in Canon 8 of the Council: "care should be taken that they abandon Hebrew practices. However, if they are not of this sort, they should certainly not be welcomed." The Fourth Lateran Council in 1215 with Canons 67-70 introduced the rule that Jews must be dressed differently from Christians.

Chinese Christians faced a similar situation in Hong Kong when Roman Catholic missionaries started their outreach in 1841. "The controversies of Chinese Christians' practice in Ancestral Worship are related to the deeper understanding of the nature of the practice, its significance to Chinese identity and the relationship between Christian belief and Chinese cultures. The conflict might have been avoided. The wisdom and experiences reflected in Romans 14:1-15:13 are still relevant in view of the various identity crisis situations in the cultural contexts of our times."[82]

If Israel developed ways to transfer blame for disobedience, then *how much more* (explicit *kal vahomer*) has the Church developed various theologies to transfer blame for its disobedience.

Difficulties in Some Books of the New Testament

The history of Biblical interpretation includes adherence to outdated or erroneous theologies, incorrect calculation of dates/the order in which the books of the New Testament were written, attributing authorship to the wrong person, a lack of knowledge of the cultural and religious background of the texts, a poor knowledge of the Old Testament, and so on. Even the goals of the writing may be misstated.

Gospel of Matthew

The Gospel of Matthew is the most challenging book to understand in the New Testament. The author's name in Greek is Matfia (Matt. 9:9), Levi (Mark 2:14), and Matityahu in Hebrew. Matthew emphasizes the fulfillment of the Old Testament prophecies in Jesus. The Gospel is neither a history book nor a detailed description of the Lord's life. The Gospel is always a theological book, based on the faith in God.

The Gospel of Matthew is written to the Jewish believers, and it is the most Jewish-centric of the four Gospels. Matthew included more direct citations from and indirect allusions to the Old Testament than any other Gospel authors. He used numbers according to the Semitic practice. The narrative is carefully divided into logical parts. For example, ten miracles and ten parables are grouped as units, letting the audience know that ten means a multitude, and imply many more than that in Jewish symbolism. The entire Gospel is divided into seven sections, and seven is the number of God in the Jewish mind. In this way Matthew emphasized that this book serves as a handbook about God. There is a prominent abundance of passages where Jesus is shown as the teacher.

82 Lo Lung-kwong, Identity Crisis Reflected in Romans 14:10 - 15:13 and the Implications for the Chinese Christians Controversy on Ancestral Worship (2002).

The use of numerous Semitisms and Hebrew literary patterns by Matthew demonstrates that he spent considerable time and was active in the Jewish community. The presence of parataxis is noticeable. It adds to the Gospel's complexity.

Unlike nowadays, there were not too many theological differences between Jewish Christians and Jews in the first century. At the time of writing, Israel was on the verge of a cataclysmic defeat in the war against Rome and the destruction of the Temple was imminent. Matthew was seeking an answer as to when his people would receive God's help.

Matthew recorded a number of prophecies made by Jesus and about Him. Why will the Temple be destroyed? The Gospel's answer is based on the rejection of Jesus Christ (Matt. 23:37-24:2).

When the whole world collapses around a man, when people are helpless, Matthew's Gospel gives people the answer: hope and purpose.

Gospel of Mark

The Gospel of Mark, the first Gospel written, serves as the framework for other synoptic Gospels. It addresses Gentile believers. Mark translates Aramaic words into Greek (Mark 5:41, 7:34, 15:34). He explains some Jewish traditions and uses far less quotations from the Old Testament than other Gospel writers. Mark applies the Roman count of time and uses some Latin words. Mark's Greek name was Ioann, or Yohanan in Hebrew.

Linguistic analysis of the prose reveals that Greek is a foreign language for Mark. It is possible to summarize this finding in two words: constant *parataxis*. Mark's writing is abundant with the "and" conjunction, which is positioned at the beginning of the sentence in most cases, emphasizing a continuous rhythm and a connection with the previous text. His Gospel is presented succinctly, and Jesus' portrayed journey could connect Galilee and Jerusalem with a straight line. Mark devotes 36% of the total narrative to these locations and events. The author also places an emphasis on the actions of the Lord, with frequent use of the word "immediately."

Mark limits his story to eighteen miracles and only four parables. The subject of the single dialogue with Jesus is His future persecutions. Jesus is called a rabbi, or "teacher" in Hebrew. Mark makes his focus the humanity of the Lord.

Mark's closing statement brings us to the story about the women who "went out and fled from the tomb, for trembling and astonishment had gripped them; and they said nothing to anyone, for they were afraid." Mark's narrative is dramatic. The women were bewildered and speechless, as Mark himself was.

The longer and shorter endings after Mark 16:8 were added much later. They do not belong to the "original autographs" and are bracketed in most versions of the Bible. Earlier texts, including two of the most important ones (Sinaiticus and Vaticanus) omit them.

The immediate response to Jesus is emphasized in the Gospel. The whole Gospel of Mark is a continuous single thought which does not shift from the main message: *Jesus Christ*.

Gospel of Luke

The prefaces to the Gospel and the Book of Acts address Theophilus (Luke 1:3, Acts 1:1). The name means "lover of God" and could fit any Christian. The narrative leads through the account of the events "that have been fulfilled among us" (Luke 1:1).

The Gospel of Luke is not just a Jewish story, but is a universal story about the Messiah of the whole world.

Many believe that if the New Testament does not mention the Jewishness of Luke, thus he must have definitely been Greek. The idea of the "Gentile" Luke took root much later, when Jewish influence started to decline in the Church. In previous chapters of this book, it was shown that Luke's Greek was influenced by the norms of the Hebrew language.

Luke demonstrates an excellent knowledge of Temple Levitical operations, not commonly known by Gentiles (Luke 1:8-20). In the original Greek text, he uses the name of the mother of Jesus, Mariam (Miryam in Hebrew), more accurately than other evangelists do.

He utilizes *kal vachomer* in the parables included in his Gospel. In all likelihood, Luke was a Jew.

The simple analysis of the frequency of *parataxis* usage confirms it. The usage of conjunctions at the beginning of the first three chapters are as follows: Matthew, 83%; Mark, 87%; Luke, 74%; John, 57%. The common frequency in the English language is 0.9%.

Luke starts introducing the parents of John the Baptist, who fill one of the most critical roles as he announces and prepares the people for their Messiah's coming and ministry. His parents' names seem to be not accidental in the narrative: Zacharias (Greek) means "God (Yehovah in Hebrew) remembers." Elizabeth (Greek) is translated as "my God is an oath." God promised and prepared Israel for the coming of her Messiah through His prophets, including John the Baptist, and delivered His salvation.

When Jesus was called to read from Scriptures at the synagogue, in His hometown, He selected Isa. 61:1 which is not a part of traditional liturgy. Then He applied *gezera shava* and said: "Today this scripture is fulfilled in your hearing" (Luke 4:16-30). Luke's Gospel starts with the scene in the Temple (Luke 1:8) and ends in the Temple (Luke 25:52).

One peculiarity of Luke's language is that he did not quote the Septuagint, but made his own translation from Hebrew (Luke 11:20):

> [20] If it is by the *finger* of God that I cast out demons, then the kingdom of God has come upon you.

The expression "finger of God" can be found in Ex. 8:19, 31:18 and Deut. 9:10. In the Septuagint, the Greek text is syntactically correct, with the definite article (τω δακτυλω του Θεου), the certain finger of the certain God. But Luke omitted the definite article, because in Hebrew, *etsba Elohim*, finger of God, is used without the definite article. Therefore, Luke not only knew the Hebrew language, but also knew the Bible in Hebrew better than the Septuagint translation.

It is very unlikely to find commentaries on the following two verses as a unit (Luke 16:16-17):

[16] The Law and the Prophets were proclaimed until John. Since that time, the good news of the kingdom of God is being preached, and everyone is forcing his way into it. [17] It is easier for heaven and earth to disappear than for the least stroke of a pen to drop out of the Law.

The first part of the Greek text in verse 16 does not have a verb. The words "forcing his way" in Greek have the meaning of "the utmost earnestness and effort." "The least stroke of a pen" in verse 17 is, in Greek, "little horn," the little part in the upper-right corner which differentiates two letters in Hebrew: resh (ר) and dalet (ד). The same word is used in Matt. 5:17-18. The following translation brings the passage closer to the author's intent:

[16] The Law and the Prophets were until John. Since that time, the good news of the kingdom of God is being proclaimed, and everyone makes an utmost effort to reach it. [17] It is easier for heaven and earth to disappear than for the smallest detail of the Law fall down.

God is faithful and none of His Law will be invalidated. The Gospel of Jesus Christ is proclaimed on the foundation of the Law and the Prophets. Therefore, Luke 16 and 17 should be interpreted only as a unit.

In the following text, Luke uses the Greek word *ethne*, "nations" (Luke 12:30):

[30] And all the nations [*Gentiles*] of the world seek after these things, and your Father knows that you need them.

However, Luke does not use it in its Greek meaning, but as the literal translation from Hebrew of the word *goyim*, Gentiles, or those who are not Jewish.

Luke uses the words "to go down from" or "to go up to" Jerusalem in the distinctive way these phrases are used in Jewish culture (Luke 18:31):

[31] And taking the twelve, he said to them, "See, we *are going up to* Jerusalem, and everything that is written about the Son of Man by the prophets will be accomplished."

For Jews, this is a religious concept rather than a geographical one. Mount Hebron is on a higher level than Jerusalem, and the Jews physically descend from it. However, they say "*go up* to Jerusalem" (but downstream by the Jordan River). After the journey they come back to the Hebron location *down* from Jerusalem.

Probably the most outrageous example of misreading a New Testament passage and envenoming it with hate may be found in the sermons against the Jews written by John Chrysostom in 386. In these eight sermons, the archbishop of Constantinople used typology, taking quotes out of context to convey an anti-Biblical message. For example, he wrote in Homilies *Adversus Judaeos*, 1:II, 6:

> Although such beasts are unfit for work, they are fit for killing. And this is what happened to the Jews: while they were making themselves unfit for work, they grew fit for slaughter. This is why Christ said: "But as for these my enemies, who did not want me to be king over them, bring them here and slay them."

This quotation was taken from Luke 19:26-27:

> [26] He replied, "I tell you that to everyone who has, more will be given, but as for the one who has nothing, even what he has will be taken away. [27] But those enemies of mine who did not want me to be king over them—bring them here and kill them in front of me."

The full text of the parable pertains to the Kingdom of God (Luke 19:11-27). Chrysostom incited Christians to kill Jews claiming that this call followed the teaching of Jesus. These homilies were referred to in the planning of the Holocaust in Hitler's Germany.

There is also a recent reference to these homilies on a website affiliated with Hamas, a U.S.-designated terrorist organization. Article 7 of The Covenant of the Islamic Resistance Movement (Hamas) of 1988 states:

The Day of Judgement will not come about until Moslems fight the Jews (killing the Jews), when the Jew will hide behind stones and trees. The stones and trees will say O Moslems, O Abdulla, there is a Jew behind me, come and kill him.

Gospel of John

John wrote his Gospel at a time when the paths of Judaism and Christianity began to part, and the Church started to lose its Jewish character. The new Gospel had to be adjusted to these new circumstances.

According to the Jewish tradition, symbolism is an indispensable part of the Gospel and can provide as much information as the text itself. Thus, seven miracles are included in the Gospel, and Jesus says "I am" seven times. In Jewish symbolism, number seven signifies the presence of God, and John did everything possible to create a Gospel with Jesus in the center.

The Gospel was written during turbulent times with the Jewish community. Moreover, this is connected with the obvious missionary emphasis of the book.

John writes of Wisdom as the manifestation of the Word of God existing before the foundation of the world (John 1:1-3):

> [1] In the beginning was the Word, and the Word was with God, and the Word was God. [2] He was with God in the beginning. [3] All things were created through him and apart from him not one thing was created that has been created.

See Ps. 33:6:

> [6] The heavens were made by the word of the Lord, and all the stars, by the breath of his mouth.

See also Prov. 3:19:

> [19] The Lord founded the earth by wisdom and established the heavens by understanding.

In his Gospel, John uses the Greek word *logos*, which relates to word, reason, etc., and is rather impersonal. In the Greek mind, *logos* is not preexistent. While writing in Greek, John brings his Jewish reasoning to express the meaning of the "word," which is the creative and directive word of God, turning it into something much weightier than the usual Greek sense of *logos*.

According to this connotation, Jesus is the personification of the divine word, God's Law (Torah), and His wisdom. The teaching on the Law (Torah) being abrogated in Church history contradicted John's witnessing of Jesus.

Acts of the Apostles

The Book of Acts is the timetable and synopsis of the development of the early Church. However, this is not just a chronicle; it is also a proclamation of triumphalist Christianity. Luke is the only author who wrote the sequel to his Gospel; there is a clear continuity from Luke 24:13 through Acts 1:15. The resurrected Jesus spent forty days with His Church (Acts 1:3). The disciples followed His command to proclaim the Gospel to everybody "starting with Jerusalem" (Luke 24:47-48). The Book of Acts is the record of God's fulfilled promises to Israel. From the beginning of the Lord's ministry up to almost twenty years after His resurrection, the Gospel message goes almost exclusively to Israel. The book of Acts reports the numbers of Jewish people saved as:

- 120 believers (Acts 1:15); this number represents the symbolic notion as 12*10 are numbers for Israel (12) and the multitude (10)
- 3,000 (Acts 2:41)
- 5,000 (Acts 4:4)
- Multitudes (Acts 6:7)
- Thousands (Acts 21:20)

During the festival of Shavuot (Pentecost), the devout "Jews from every nation under heaven" (Acts 2:5) became witnesses of the gift of the tongues given to the disciples. Common teaching interprets this day as the birthday of the Church. Before the events of Pentecost, Jesus' disciples represented the First Church when they shared the first communion (Matt. 26: 26-28) and received the Holy Spirit (John 20:22).

The priority of Jewish evangelism was mandated by Jesus (Matt. 10:5-7, 15:24). Moreover, it is stipulated in many of the letters in the New Testament. The major break with this focus occurs when the Gospel begins to go to the Gentiles, starting with the baptism of the Ethiopian eunuch (Acts 8:26-39) and the narrative about the centurion Cornelius

(Acts 10). Following God's promise that He would bless all nations through Abraham (Gen. 12:3) the Council (Acts 15) concluded that Gentiles could follow Jesus without converting to Judaism. Luke shows the unity of the Church and the unity of doctrine.

At the end of his journeys Paul returned to Jerusalem, where he completed his Nazirite oath (Acts 21:20-26). After that, Paul faced accusation and conspiracy from the High Priest, was arrested, and then saved by the Roman soldiers. Accusations were presented of numerous violations of the Law of Moses. Paul defended himself in Acts 24:12-15:

> [12] My accusers did not find me arguing with anyone at the temple, or stirring up a crowd in the synagogues or anywhere else in the city. [13] And they cannot prove to you the charges they are now making against me. [14] However, I admit that I worship the God of our fathers as a follower of the Way, which they call a sect. I believe everything that agrees with the Law and that is written in the Prophets, [15] and I have the same hope in God as these men, that there will be a resurrection of both the righteous and the wicked.

During that time Christianity spread from the religious center in Jerusalem to the center of the Roman Empire.

1 Corinthians

Only two of many letters to Corinth are known. A diverse array of topics are presented in Paul's letters, along with admonitions to different groups of Corinthian Christians. Paul was disconcerted as his authority and spiritual warnings were questioned by the Church in Corinth. Both letters to Corinth present a strong opposition to the spiritual situation and teachings of the Church there.

Many of the so-called "new" challenges faced by the contemporary Church are startlingly similar to those described by Paul. His words are based on the position of Jesus.

The following is Paul's admonition on the Law of Moses for Gentiles in the Church (1 Cor. 7:19):

> [19] Circumcision is nothing and uncircumcision is nothing. Keeping God's commands is what counts.

He teaches on the need to preach the Gospel to Jews, 1 Cor. 14:21:

> [21] In the Law it is written: "Through men of strange tongues and through the lips of foreigners I will speak to this people..."[83]

Paul points to Jesus who brought Israel out of Egypt (1 Cor. 10:1-4):

> [1] And I do not want you to be ignorant, brothers, that our forefathers were all under the cloud and that they all passed through the sea. [2] They were all *baptized* into Moses in the cloud and in the sea. [3] They all ate the same spiritual food [4] and drank the same spiritual drink, and they drank from the spiritual rock that walked with them, and that rock was *Christ*.

It might be assumed that Jesus also gave the Law to Moses.

Paul advised the Church as follows (1 Cor. 10:31):

> [32] And to Jews, and Greeks, and the church of God, give no offense.

He concludes (1 Cor. 16:13-14):

> [13] Be on your guard; stand firm in the faith; be men of courage; be strong. [14] Do everything in love.

The Apostle articulated a very important idea when he addressed Christians, the former unbelieving Gentiles (1 Cor. 12:2):

> [2] You know that *when you were Gentiles...*

2 Corinthians

Paul addresses persistent tensions caused by his opponents over the exercise of his ministry. He rebukes non-Biblical teaching of the Gospel, which he calls another Gospel (2 Cor. 11:13-15):

> [13] And such men are false apostles, deceitful workmen, masquerading as apostles of Christ. [14] And no wonder, and Satan himself masquerades as an angel of light. [15] And it is not surprising, then, if his servants masquerade as servants of righteousness. And their end will be what their actions deserve.

---

83 Isa. 28:11.

Paul's readers were familiar with the Jewish festival of *Sukkot*, when Israelites built and dwelled in *sukkahs* for seven days (Lev. 23:43). Paul made the analogy of a human body to a *sukkah* being a very transient dwelling place. Believers will move from the temporary to the permanent; from a flimsy tent to an eternal house in heavens (2 Cor. 5:1, 4):

> [1] And we know that if the earthly shelter, sukkah, is destroyed, we have a building from God, an eternal house in heaven, not built by human hands...
>
> [4] And while we are in this sukkah, we groan and are burdened, because we do not wish to be unclothed but to be clothed with our heavenly dwelling, so that what is mortal may be swallowed up by life.

Paul taught the way to resolve the Church's conflict in 2 Cor. 6:14-17:

> [14] Do not be unequally yoked with unbelievers. For what do righteousness and what without the Law have in common? Or what fellowship can light have with darkness? [15] What harmony is there between Christ and Belial? What does a believer have in common with an unbeliever? [16] What agreement is there between the Temple of God and idols? And we are the Temple of the living God. As God has said: "I will live with them and walk among them, and I will be their God, and they will be my people. [17] Therefore come out from them and be separate, says the Lord. And do not touch unclean thing, and I will receive you.

When unbelievers violate the Mosaic Law, they are not righteous.

Galatians

Galatian Churches were comprised mainly of Gentile converts (Gal. 4:8). Some congregants led the Churches astray from Paul's faith-centered teaching to obtain salvation by "works of the Law." They claimed that Paul's teaching was not sufficient, and that they should embrace Judaism. Moreover, since they became believers less than three years before the letter's writing, they still held some of their beliefs in the pagan gods (Gal. 4:8-10). As a result, those Galatians adhered to a mixture of Christianity, Judaism, and idolatry. Thus, they practiced not monotheism, but polytheism mixed with syncretism.

After they accepted Judaism, Galatians were required to keep all commandments. However, they did not understand the essence and purpose of the Law, and they unknowingly committed new sins. Their decisions were made on the basis of a very limited knowledge and led to unforeseen consequences.

Paul selected two texts that speak of both righteousness and faith together: Gen. 15:6 in Gal. 3:6 and Hab. 2:4 in Gal. 3:11. When they became believers and obeyed those commandments, then they were righteous according to the definition of Mosaic Law.

Being Messiah followers and righteous, they are called saints in the New Testament. Therefore, they have all the blessings which are promised to the descendants of Abraham in Gen. 12:2-3, and they do not require a process of obtaining righteousness.

Paul's point of view could be summarized as: Jesus already accepted the Gentile believers as part of Israel (Gal. 3:29):

> [29] If you belong to Christ, then you *are Abraham's seed*, and heirs according to the promise.

Using the analogy, we question if there is a need to falsify the document of the will and testament, while you are the sole benefactor. If someone forges it, then it would lose its power.

It is particularly important to understand what Paul *knew, but did not say, because he believed it was obvious*. That knowledge was the basis of the letter, but it is implicit, not explicit. It can only be found by understanding Paul's ideas and his character. Understanding the Jewish roots of the New Testament is necessary. Any attempt to interpret the Epistle otherwise will inevitably be based on the commentator's experience and knowledge rather than Paul's.

The letter was written *after* the Jerusalem Council's decision that Gentiles should not be converted to Judaism but should keep a few commandments of the Law (Acts 15:28-29). Therefore, the decision of Galatians, among other things, creates a challenge to the authority of the First Church.

Ephesians

Paul's message of the high calling (Eph. 1-3) makes it critical to extort the Church in Ephesus to maintain the unity, especially between Jewish and Gentile believers united in the Messiah. Believing Gentiles are brought into the commonwealth of Israel (Eph. 2:11-22). It implies an obligation to relate as family in the body of Messiah (Eph. 2:12-13). According to Paul, they did not fully understand the Jewish roots of their faith and should be in union with Jewish believers (Eph. 4:1-16, 32). At the time, the Ephesians were prepared to accept what was previously too difficult for them. Paul's primary call is in Eph. 5:1-2:

> [1] Be imitators of God, therefore, as dearly loved children [2] and live a life of love, just as Christ loved us and gave himself up for us as a fragrant offering and sacrifice to God.

This message is still relevant for the contemporary Church.

Philippians

The story of the Church's creation in Philippi stands out. Paul arrived at the small town of Roman settlers (Acts 16:12) and found neither Jews nor a synagogue there. But he shared the Gospel with some women at the riverside on the Sabbath day (Acts 16:13-15). Only Lydia and her household received the Lord and were baptized. Lydia was originally from Thyatira, which had dyeing facilities and was a center of the cloth trade. Later, the head of the prison and his household joined in faith (Acts 16:21-33). Paul departed and wrote his letter eleven years later to the now-thriving Church. Unlike other early Churches outside Judea, this congregation did not include any Jewish believers.

1 Thessalonians

In all likelihood, this letter is the earliest of Paul's epistles to new believers, composed in roughly 51 A.D. The young congregation was founded less than a year before this writing.

The text in 1 Thess. 4:13-17 states that all those who are already dead will be resurrected first, speaking of the saints of the Old and New Testaments: "For the Lord himself will descend with the loud command, the voice of the Archangel, and with God's trumpet [*shofar*]," and only then the believers will be taken into the clouds to meet the Lord.

Titus

Of particular interest today is the use of the words *presbyteros* (Titus 1:5), and *presbytēs/presbytis* (Titus 2:2, 3), elders and old men. The word *presbyteros* stands for the older people. Usually *presbyteros* are identified with power, and *presbytēs* with age. However, in the Septuagint the word *presbytēs* may have both meanings; it is identified with authority in 2 Chron. 32:31, 1 Macc. 14:22, 15:17, 2 Macc. 11:34, Job 29:7-8, and in Lam. 5:14 it was identified with authority. Paul calls himself *presbytēs*, Phile. 9.

The Law of Moses is mentioned three times in the letter (Titus 2:14, 3:9). A common incorrect translation may be found in Titus 3:13, where all Bible versions list Zenas as a lawyer. Some commentaries designate him as an attorney. In the ancient world, occupations such as lawyer, attorney, or barrister did not exist. The Greek word is *nomikos*, derived from *nomos*, the Law of Moses, and should be translated as "expert in the Law of Moses." The word *nomikos* is used in the New Testament in Matt. 22:35, Luke 7:30, 10:25, 11:45, 46, 52, 14:3, Titus 3:9, and sometimes it is translated correctly, Luke 7:30 (NIV):

> [30] But the Pharisees and *experts in the Law* rejected God's purpose for themselves...

The correct translation of Titus 3:13 is as follows:

> [13] Do everything you can to help *the experts in the Mosaic Law* Zenas and Apollos on their way...

Zenas and Apollos were Jews with Greek names. For Paul, being an expert in the Law was a valuable qualification.

Philemon

This Epistle is small and private, with a request to take back a fugitive slave and accept him as a Christian, but the value of this epistle is incomparable. It points to the egalitarian aspect of the Bible, that *all* people have the same intrinsic value for God and for all believers regardless of race, sex, or social class.

Hebrews

This Epistle presents a deep knowledge of (and numerous quotations from and allusions to) the Old Testament. Most likely, the author was a well-educated, bilingual Jew. Based on linguistic analysis, his Epistle demonstrates the best Greek prose found in the New Testament. Neither the writing style, nor the polished Greek composition support Pauline authorship.

The Jews living in the Roman provinces left 76% of their general records in Greek, 23% in Latin and only 1% in Hebrew. The text includes some Latin words that were then in common use in southern Italy.

The suggestion that intended readers were mostly Gentile believers has merit (Heb. 5:11-14, 6:1-2). The quotations in the letter are given only from the Septuagint; in all likelihood, the addressees studied Scripture in Greek.

The events referred to in the Epistle might have taken place just before the destruction of the Second Temple. The Jewish and Gentile Christians worshiped in the Temple; the latter did it in the Court of Gentiles. In Judaism the loss of the Temple may be replaced by the services in the synagogues. At the time the majority of Jews already lived in the diaspora outside of Judea and many of them had never visited the Temple.

The goal of the author is to answer the question: "How will believers live without the Temple?" The Epistle answers the question in a unique way based on the exceptional nature of the unique Lord, Jesus Christ. The author constantly uses *kal vachomer* in each chapter to prove his point; e.g., if Jesus is superior to...then *how much more* is the heavenly original Temple "not made by hands" (Heb. 9:23-24) better than the earthly Temple. The original heavenly Temple is preserved in heaven, and only its imperfect earthly copy will be destroyed, but the Shekhinah, the glory of God, will never depart from this Temple in heaven.

The other theme of the Epistle is the need for a response to the number of Christians who fell away from the Church in the time of persecutions, but later were willing to return (Heb. 6:4-8). At that time Jewish believers were considered by Romans to be the part of a new branch within diaspora Judaism. Since Judaism was perceived as an established and acceptable religion, only Gentile Christians were persecuted by the emperor. Thus, the epistle addresses mostly non-Jewish believers.

The description of the events found in Mark 11:12-21 and Matt. 21:12-21 tells us about the future destruction of the Temple.

The Church accepted the value of the themes and included the epistle into the canon of the New Testament. Only much later, while the Jewish roots of Christianity were being overlooked, did the Church do the same with the existence of the heavenly Jewish Temple.

1 Peter

When seeing the word dispersion, *diaspora* in Greek, everyone begins to think about the Jews. However, in 1 Peter 2:10 and 4:3-4 we find that the addressees were Gentile Christians. Peter, like other Biblical authors, included them in Israel.

The purpose of the letter is to prepare the former pagans for the future persecutions because of their faith. Their lives must be impeccable among Gentiles, in other words, among pagans. This teaching is consistent with defining the addressees as aliens and strangers in 1 Peter 2:11, in Hebrew *ger toshav*. Nowadays Jewish people add an additional meaning to the word: a *friend*.

In 1 Peter 4:6 the statement that the dead have already heard the Gospel alleviates grief upon the loss of loved ones.

Finally, the elders of the Churches must be impeccable even among the impeccable (1 Peter 5:1-3).

2 Peter

Peter's writing in Greek is sometimes inflected by Hebrew expressions, e.g., "to fall out of secure steadfastness," "burning flames," "last days," "sons of curse," "to unbind the prophecy," etc. The Law of Moses is also mentioned twice in 2 Peter 2:8, 16, and in both cases the original Greek was deliberately altered. Peter blames the unbelieving members of the Church for the violation of Mosaic Law, and he compares them with the false prophets of Israel, leaving no doubt that he writes specifically to Gentile Christians. Peter's advice is quite simple in 2 Peter 3:14:

> [14] Do everything you can to be found by Him without spot or defect and at peace [with God].

1 John

New teachings arose forty years after the beginning of the Church, and according to John they came straight from antichrists (John 3:18):

> [18] Children, it is the last hour. And as you have heard that antichrist is coming, even now many antichrists have come. By this we know that it is the last hour. [19] They went out from us, but they did not belong to us; for if they had belonged to us, they would have remained with us. However, they went out so that it might be made clear that none of them belongs to us.

John wrote about several ways of identifying them in 1 John 2:9, 3:4, 3:7-10. His teaching in 1 John 4:20-21 parallels Paul's in Rom. 14-15:

> [20] If anyone says, "I love God," and yet hates his brother or sister, he is a liar. For the person who does not love his brother or sister whom he has seen cannot love God whom he has not seen. [21] And we have this command from him: The one who loves God must also love his brother and sister.

Revelation

The Book of Revelation presents the genre of prophetic Jewish writings and apocalyptic literature. Apocalyptic writings include vivid imagery, illustrations, and symbolism. The Book of Revelation stands out as a very great challenge for interpretation, and is often misunderstood. The reader observes the dual character of Biblical prophecy; while prophesying the future, the writer describes current events and persecution of believers. The authors used the apocalyptic style with the intention of bringing more weight to their writing. The other reason was the fear of persecutions.

At the time of writing, John was the only survivor out of the twelve original disciples of the Messiah. Domitian, the emperor of Rome, exiled John to the island of Patmos. Revelation was written before the time of the emperor's death at the age of forty-four. Two years later, at the age of eighty-seven, John died as a free man. The author intended to equip believers for living through a time of trials.

The distinctive character of the book means that it contains more quotations from the Old Testament, as well as images and illustrations from Scripture, than all other books of the New Testament.

An analysis of the Greek language of the Book of Revelation shows that it is grammatically simple, with only a few complex words and exhibiting a strong influence from the Hebrew language.

Some commentators name them as solecisms and argue about the purpose of the irregular Greek language in Revelation and John's disregard of the original meaning.[84] The possibility of changing the meaning of the original text in a quotation was mentioned in this book on page 123. Additionally, when the presence of the rule *gezera shava* (explained on pp. 41-45) is not taken into consideration, the commentators conclude that the quoting is out of context. Since John's native language was first-century Hebrew, the modern idea of preserving the text and context of a quotation was unknown to him.

One of the challenging interpretations comes from the message to seven Churches in Revelation. The commentators suggested that allegory was the key to unlock Revelation, and seven Churches represented seven periods of history. When we apply the Jewish background to the interpretation of the message, we would see the singular message to the Churches with their different problems. This approach would help to single out the letter to Thyatira. According to Tertulian and Epiphanius, the Church in Thyatira did not yet exist at the time of writing.[85] That was supported by Edward Gibbon.[86]

The imagery of the mark of the beast, Rev. 13:16-18, signifies loy-

---

84 G.K. Beale, John's Use of the Old Testament in Revelation (1998) 138.

85 Ethelbert W. Bullinger, Commentary on Revelation: A Classic Evangelical Commentary (1902, 2004) 70.

86 Edward Gibbon, The History of The Decline and Fall of The Roman Empire (1776).

alty. It is the indirect proof that the Rapture of believers will not occur before the advent of the anti-Messiah. What is the use of marking all of the population, when God's people are gone? The verses in Rev. 7:9-14 made the claim of the "pre-trib" even more unfounded. John continues to describe the persecution of Christians in the latter part of the first century, Rev. 7:9. God considers Christians to be worthy of His care.

John completes the book by quoting the Mosaic Law in Rev. 22:18-19:

> [18] I warn everyone who hears the words of the prophecy of this book: If anyone adds anything to them, God will add to him the plagues described in this book. [19] And if anyone takes words away from this book of prophecy, God will take away from him his share in the tree of life and in the holy city, which are described in this book.

The single verse in Deut. 12:32 includes two commandments:

> [32] Be careful to keep every word I command you; do not add above to it, and not take away from it.

Conclusion

The mission of the Church was to share the faith and teaching of Christ, but Christ and Biblical truth are no longer the driving force and foundation in the Church.[87]

The New Testament is a thoroughly Jewish book written by Jewish authors. It demonstrates God's grace and inclusion extended to the entire world through faith in the Jewish Messiah. Transitioning from interpreting the Scriptures through the Greek mindset in its history, the Church should become more attuned to the Hebraic mindset of the Bible. "Without a thorough knowledge of history, men and women can neither fully understand themselves nor make wise choices for their present and future."[88] When the student of the Scriptures establishes what the text was saying to its original readers, a real feel for the issues addressed can be developed. Only then are students ready for the stage of personal or group application.

Interpreting the New Testament through the lens of the source Scriptures (Old Testament), becoming familiar with the Semitic reasoning of the authors and the linguistic, cultural, and historical settings of the text, brings the reader to a better knowledge of the Bible and a stronger relationship with God.

---

87 Harold L. Senkbeil, Lucas V. Woodford, Brian Croft, Pastoral Leadership: For the Care of Souls (2021) 46, 169.

88 Robert Michael, Holy Hatred: Christianity, Antisemitism, and the Holocaust (2006).

Printed in the USA
CPSIA information can be obtained
at www.ICGtesting.com
LVHW051345011224
797933LV00013B/1201